Theo Chester

Stray Dogs

Salamander Street

PLAYS

First published by in 2023 by Salamander Street Ltd., a Wordville imprint.
(info@salamanderstreetcom).

Stray Dogs © Theo Chester, 2023

Cover illustration by Guy Saunders.

ISBN: 9781914228858

10 9 8 7 6 5 4 3 2 1

Further copies of this publication can be purchased from
www.salamanderstreet.com

Stray Dogs was first performed at Theatre503 in London on 14th March 2023. The cast was as follows:

Jacob	Graham Butler
Hilde	Abbey Gillett
Franz/Pig	Graeme McKnight
Ana	Ruxandra Porojnicu
Wilf	Coral Wylie

Casting Director	Amy Blair
Writer	Theo Chester
Production Manager	Emily Dickson
Director	Tommo Fowler
Creative Access Consultant	Aisling Gallagher
Sound Designer	Jose Guillermo Puello
Dramaturg	Frey Kwa-Hawking
Set and Costume Designer	Anna Lewis
Lighting Designer	Megan Lucas
Producer	Cindy McLean-Bibby
Marketing Coordinator	Hayley Salter
Stage Manager	Sussan Sanii
Graphic Designer	Guy Saunders
Assistant Director	Elsa Strachan

CAST

Graham Butler – Jacob – He/Him

Graham trained at Guildhall School of Music & Drama.

Theatre credits include: *Cleansed, The White Guard* (National Theatre); *The Curious Incident of the Dog in the Night-Time* (Gielgud Theatre/National Theatre); *Journey's End* (West End/National Tour); *Henry VI Parts 1,2,3, Henry V, Richard II, Nell Gwynne* (Shakespeare's Globe); *Sweet Bird of Youth* (Chichester Festival Theatre); *The Cherry Orchard* (Nottingham Playhouse).

TV credits include: *Doctor Who* (BBC); *Bancroft* (ITV); *Penny Dreadful 1 & 2* (Showtime/Sky); *Suspects* (Channel 5/Freemantle).

Film credits include: *The Isle* (Great Point Media); *Two Down* (Fizz and Ginger Films); *Bright Star* (BBC Film).

Abbey Gillett – Hilde – She/Her

Abbey trained at LAMDA and Tring Park School for the Performing Arts.

Theatre credits include: *Macbeth* (RABBLE Theatre).

Training credits include: *Faustus: That Damned Woman, The Welkin, Mr Burns: A Post-Electric Play, A Midsummer Night's Dream, Sorry You're Not a Winner* (Workshop - Paines Plough), *Cymbeline, Children of the Sun.*

Graeme McKnight – Franz/Pig – He/Him

Graeme trained at RADA.

Theatre credits include: *Our Country's Good, Comedy of Errors* (National Theatre); *Silent Planet* (Finborough Theatre); *The Tempest* (Norwich and Norfolk Festival); *Penetrator* (GBS Theatre).

Television credits include: *Hijack* (Apple TV); *Outlander* (Starz Entertainment); *The Walk In* (ITV Studios); *Mr. Selfridge* (ITV Studios); *Outlaws* (BBC/Hartswood Films).

Films credits include: *Death Defying Acts* (Zephyr Films); *Dark Sense* (Encaptivate).

Ruxandra Porojnicu – Ana – She/Her

Ruxandra is making her London stage debut with *Stray Dogs*.

Television credits include: *Coronation Street* (ITV).

Film credits include: upcoming *Sumotherhood* (Paramount Pictures) written and directed by Bafta winning actor Adam Deacon.

Coral Wylie – Wilf – They/Them

Coral is a writer and actor. In 2022, Coral was awarded a place on Soho Theatre Writer's Lab, and in November it was announced they would be joining the Bush Theatre's Emerging Writer's Group for 2023.

Theatre credits include: *ANTHEM* (Bush Theatre).

CREATIVE TEAM

Amy Blair – Casting Director – She/Her

Amy is a casting director working across theatre and screen. Credits include: *Milk & Gall* (Theatre503); *Margin* (Grey Moth Films); *A Gig for Ghosts* (45 North); *Crude* (Unleyek); *Talking About a Revolution* (Tiata Fahodzi); *Slay & Prepare the Animal for Meat* (White Stag Films / Buccaneer Media); *Daddy Issues* (Liam Gartland Productions).

Theo Chester – Writer – He/Him

Theo Chester is a playwright based in London. He has been a member of Soho Theatre's Writer's Lab and Writer's Alumni Group. *Stray Dogs* is his debut play. Alongside writing he has worked in documentaries, assistant directing *Summer in the Forest* (2017). He is also training to be an English teacher.

Emily Dickson – Production Manager - She/Her

Emily studied an M.A in Collaborative Theatre Production and Design at Guildhall School of Music and Drama.

Production manager credits include: *My Brother's Keeper* (Theatre503); *CASH MONEY NOW!* (The Big House) and *run Rabbit run* (Levantes Dance Theatre, UK Tour).

Stage manager credits include: *1797: The Mariner's Revenge* (HistoryRiot) and *Mosquitoes* (OVO Theatre).

Tommo Fowler – Director – He/Him

Tommo is a freelance director and dramaturg for text and production, based in Sheffield.

He is Literary Associate of the Women's Prize for Playwriting, Co-founder of RoughHewn dramaturgy company and a Board Member of the Dramaturgs' Network. He was previously Residencies Dramaturg and a Supported Artist at Sheffield Theatres.

Directing credits include: *Jam, I Wish To Die Singing, Obama-ology* (Finborough Theatre); *How to Make a Revolution* (Finborough Online); *Mumburger* (Old Red Lion Theatre); *Comet* (Pleasance London); *The Strip* and *Fear and Misery of the Third Reich* (Oxford School of Drama).

Dramaturgy credits include: *Jews. In Their Own Words* (Royal Court); *There Is No Planet B* (Theatre Deli, Sheffield); *One Jewish Boy* (Trafalgar Studios); *Out of the Dark* (Rose Theatre, Kingston); *In My Lungs the Ocean Swells* (VAULT Festival, Origins Award Winner).

Awards: Olwen Wymark Award (Writers' Guild of Great Britain), for RoughHewn.

Aisling Gallagher – Creative Access Consultant - They/Them

Aisling Gallagher is an Irish director, artist and creative access practitioner who makes work that disrupts what is considered normal, assumed and appropriate.

Creative access consultant credits include: *Drive Your Plow Over the Bones of the Dead* (Complicità); *Stray Dogs* (Theatre503); *Fantastically Great Women Who Changed the World* (Kenny Wax/Southampton MAST); *No Mad* (Arcola).

Directing credits include: *Where the Magic Happens* (Lyric Hammersmith); *Illusions of Liberty* (Applecart Arts/King's Head).

Assisting credits include: *Fantastically Great Women Who Changed the World* (Kenny Wax/Southampton MAST).

Lead artist/residency credits include: Tyre Pressure Laboratory for Liberty Festival 2022 (Spare Tyre); Resident Artist (Theatre Centre); Sonic Conditions (Festival Echoes residency with Good Behaviour for Festival Stoke); Safe & Sound (with Good Behaviour for Sydenham Arts).

Frey Kwa Hawking – Dramaturg – He/Him

Frey Kwa Hawking is a dramaturg and theatre critic. He was Dramaturg Assistant for the Young Vic's Neighbourhood Voices programme in 2020-21, part of Paines Plough and 45North's Re:Assemble cohort for Dramaturgy practice, and trained as part of the Royal Court's 2019 Script Panel.

Dramaturg credits include: *Sundown Kiki* (Young Vic); *Andromeda* (Camden People's Theatre); *In the Net* (Jermyn Street Theatre); *Mr Brightside* (Greenwich Theatre).

Writer credits include: *Asian Pirate Musical* (Vault Festival); *Death Grip* (Michael Pilch Studio).

Anna Lewis – Set and Costume Designer – She/Her

Anna is an award-winning Set and Costume designer. She also works as a Costume Supervisor.

Design Credits include: *PRIMA* (Royal Opera House); *Amna* (Tara Theatre); *Anna Bella Eema* (Arcola Theatre); *The Marriage of Alice B Toklas* (Jermyn Street Theatre); *Carmen, Outlying Islands* and *EAST* (all Kings Head Theatre); *A Christmas Carol* (Reading Rep Theatre); *Life According to Saki* (Edinburgh Festival, Fourth Street Theatre New York); *Deadly Dialogues* (Edinburgh Festival, 3LD New York).

Costume Supervisor credits include: *we're here because we're here* (National Theatre, Birmingham Rep, 1418NOW); *Wuthering Heights* (Bristol Old Vic, National Theatre, National and International Tour); *Straight Line Crazy* (Bridge Theatre); *The Book of Dust* (Bridge Theatre).

Megan Lucas – Lighting Designer – She/Her

Megan is a lighting and video designer. She has a personal interest in accessible theatre and as a result she developed and programmed the hard-of-hearing captioning system currently in use at Royal & Derngate, Northampton. She also collaborated with the same venue to create the NextGen: Lighting Design course, giving young people an introduction to the technical and creative skills involved in stage lighting.

Lighting Designer credits include: *Past Life* (The Lowry/UK Tour); *The Hidden Garden* (National Opera Studio); *Edie* (Theatre503); *Criptic Pit Party* (The Barbican); *The Masks We Wear* (Royal and Derngate).

Assistant Lighting Designer credits include: *How The Other Half Loves* (Salisbury Playhouse); *Much Ado About Nothing* (National Theatre); *Alcina* (Glyndebourne).

Video Designer credits include: *We Started To Sing* (Arcola Theatre); *The Wellspring* (Royal and Derngate/UK Tour).

LX Programmer credits include: *Jack And The Beanstalk* (Royal and Derngate); *Playtime* (Royal and Derngate).

Cindy McLean-Bibby – Producer – She/Her

Cindy is an arts producer based in London. She currently works as the Tour Producer at Little Angel Theatre, where her recent work includes: *I Want My Hat Back Trilogy*, and the national tours of *We're Going On A Bear Hunt* and *There's a Rang-Tan In My Bedroom*. Previously, she worked at Omnibus Theatre as producer and is a co-founder of Blindside Theatre.

Theatre credits as producer include: *Skin Tight* (The Hope Theatre); *Tell 'Em* (Peckham Springs & 2Northdown); *Admissions* (Rehearsed Reading); *Changing Partners* (Brighton Fringe Festival). As associate: *Target Man* (King's Head Theatre).

Jose Guillermo Puello – Sound Designer – He/Him

Jose Guillermo Puello is a composer and sound designer from the Dominican Republic, based in Manchester. This will be his first show at

Theatre503 and he is excited to work with the creative and production teams.

Composition credits include: *Aqui/Alla* (OperaNorth); *La sombra* (Manchester Chamber Choir); *Eolicamente* (Mason&Ruttllant Duo); *Alabanzas* (Dominican National Youth Orchetra); *Cocologna* (Vaganza); *Cinquillamente* (The Fourth Wall Ensemble); *y punto* (Manchester Camerata).

Sound designer credits include: *There's No Planet B* (Theatre Deli); *Omega* (Wireless Theatre Company); *Legacy* (Royal Exchange Theatre); *The Return* (HOME).

Assistant sound designer credits include: *Rock, Paper, Scissors* (Sheffield Theatres).

Music for dance credits include: *Lonely Cities (*Rambert Studio); *Hiatus, M.E.N.* (Contact Theatre).

Awards include: National Music Prize (Dominican Republic)

Hayley Salter- Marketing Coordinator – She/Her

Hayley is a producer and arts marketer. She is also a photographer, specialising in portraiture, headshots and documentary work.

Photography and film credits include: *Photography Prize Exhibition 2023* (Royal Birmingham Society of Artists); *Reworlding* (an immersive visual arts commission at Centrala Space, Birmingham); *4600 Gifts* (Craftspace); *Out Out* (Highly Sprung Performance, Sky Arts); *Gallery 37 Residency and Exhibition* (Grain Photography Hub); *Year of the Nurse* (Florence Nightingale Museum, London).

Photography and film credits include: *Photography Prize Exhibition 2023* (Royal Birmingham Society of Artists); *Reworlding* (an immersive visual arts commission at Centrala Space, Birmingham); *4600 Gifts* (Craftspace); *Out Out* (Highly Sprung Performance, Sky Arts); *Gallery 37 Residency and Exhibition* (Grain Photography Hub); *Year of the Nurse* (Florence Nightingale Museum, London). Recent marketing work includes: *As We Speak* (Birmingham 2022 Festival); *CastAway* (Highly Sprung Performance, UK Tour); *BE Festival 2022* (REP Birmingham). Hayley studied at Goldsmiths, University of London.

Sussan Sanii – Stage Manager – She/Her

Sussan is a stage manager from Florence, Italy, of American and Iranian heritage.

Stage Manager on book credits include: *Our Streets* (Tara Theatre); *The Octopus* (Kings Head Theatre); *Angel* (WaterRats).

DSM credits include: *Aladdin, Cinderella* (Kenneth More Theatre).

ASM credits include: *Athena, The Cherry Orchard* (The Yard Theatre).

ASM on book credits include: *There is a War, Banana Boys, Great Britain and Revolt. She Said. Revolt Again* (Italia Conti Academy).

Elsa Strachan – Assistant Director – She/Her

Elsa Strachan is a theatre director from Aberdeenshire; her childhood was spent on a sheep farm, which came in surprisingly useful in the *Stray Dogs* rehearsal room.

In her work she is interested in stories about complex human relationships and graduated from the MA directing course at Rose Bruford in 2023.

Directing credits include: *Life in the Hyphen* (R&D); *Dismantling the Reindeer* (Pomona Theatre); *Blood* (Short Film).

Assistant directing credits include: *3 Winters, Phaedra* (Rose Bruford College); *A Midsummer Night's Dream* (TCP); *Alice in Wonderland* (Bell Theatre).

Theatre503 is at the forefront of identifying and nurturing new voices at the very start of their careers and launching them into the industry. They stage more early career playwrights than any other theatre in the world – with over 120 writers premiered each year from festivals of short pieces to full length productions, resulting in employment for over 1,000 freelance artists through their year-round programme.

Theatre503 provides a diverse pipeline of talent resulting in modern classics like *The Mountaintop* by Katori Hall and *Rotterdam* by Jon Brittain – both Olivier Award winners – to future classics like Yasmin Joseph's *J'Ouvert*, winner of the 2020 James Tait Black Prize and transferred to the West End/BBC Arts and *Wolfie* by Ross Willis, winner of the 2020 Writers Guild Award for Best New Play. Writers who began their creative life at Theatre503 are now writing for the likes of *The Crown*, *Succession*, *Doctor Who*, *Killing Eve* and *Normal People* and every single major subsidised theatre in the country now boasts a new play by a writer who started at Theatre503.

THEATRE503 TEAM

Artistic Director	Lisa Spirling
Interim Executive Director	Jules Oakshett
Literary Manager	Steve Harper
Producer	Ceri Lothian
General Manager	Tash Berg
Carne Associate Director	Jade Lewis
Literary Associate	Lauretta Barrow
Trainee Assistant Producers	Catherine Moriarty, Tsipora St. Clair Knights
Technical Manager	Misha Mah
Marketing Officer	Millie Whittam
Administrator	Lizzie Akita
Development Coordinator	Heloise Gillingham

CHARACTERS

Jacob (pronounced Yakob)

Hilde (pronounced Hillder)

Ana

Franz

Wilf

Pig

SETTING

A small walled city in central europe,
inside and outside the walls

Woods

Prison cells

Houses

Tents

OBJECTS

An executioner's sword - a sword with both edges
sharp and a sqaure end.

NOTES

Add pauses when they feel right for you.

1.

Inside the walls.

A room.

Franz *has his mouth open.*

Jacob *spits on his hands.*

Jacob *hesitates.*

JACOB: Little wider.

Franz *opens his mouth a little wider.*

Little more.

Franz *opens his mouth wider, cries out in pain, flinches.*

FRANZ: Trying to make my head split in two?

JACOB: Know it hurts.

Franz *opens as wide as possible, in spite of the pain.*

Jacob *peers into* **Franz's** *mouth, reaches in, touches.* **Franz** *holds still.*

Jacob *sees what he needs to see.*

He gestures for **Franz** *to close his mouth.*

FRANZ: Well?

A moment.

JACOB: Needs pulling.

FRANZ: That's your way?

JACOB: Best thing. Cleanest thing.

FRANZ: No.

JACOB: Sir-

FRANZ: Jon, rich and blessed merchant, dead last year of a pulled tooth. My own mother almost lost her life. Another pulled tooth.

JACOB: If it gets further -

FRANZ: You catch me spitting pain and say you've a way, a way to fix this, own special way, you.

So.

What is it?

A moment.

JACOB: Salt. The grit of it. Rub it into your gums.

FRANZ: Like I'm a piece of pork?

JACOB: Binds a poor sinner's wounds well enough.

Use it after I've been with them in the cells.

FRANZ: That's how they look half way to heavenly?

JACOB: Trick of father's.

Wherever've been. Whatever've done. Use salt on them all.

FRANZ: How often with this salt?

JACOB: Twice a day.

FRANZ: Must work.

JACOB: Will.

FRANZ: Better. This winter may've taken grain, sheep, herdsmen, but it'll not take my tooth and life along with it.

JACOB: Cold can't take a tooth.

FRANZ: I've a new book on the body, the way it decays. Says that rot comes on the air.

The men, women, children, sheep, starved by the cold, their rot floats over the town walls. Straight into my tooth.

JACOB: Their bodies?

FRANZ: Rot from their bodies. Wish I could blow it away.

JACOB: Have to stop them dying.

FRANZ: You'd need a cure for hunger and cold.

JACOB: Fire and food.

FRANZ: In limited supply, specially now.

Unless you've a hoard of grain under your house?

JACOB: But.

FRANZ: What?

JACOB: Give you my report?

FRANZ: Back to business.

Alright.

JACOB: Peaceful. Everything's peaceful.

FRANZ: Good.

JACOB: Has been peaceful all through winter.

FRANZ: One herdsman slipped through the gates and stole.

JACOB: Only one.

Herdsmen outside could do all kinds of things. But they don't.

FRANZ: Cos you hang them.

JACOB: Doesn't stop others slipping over and stuffing their pockets with grain from the merchants' cellars.

FRANZ: They've a bit of intelligence in them is why.

JACOB: Hunger makes you stupid.

FRANZ: Schooling me?

JACOB: No sir.

FRANZ: Are.

If I'd given the herdsmen grain from merchants' stores, all the sheep'd be dead and what then of the wool, milk, meat, the coin they bring? Be nothing for anyone, least of all the herdsmen. They know this.

JACOB: Feeding sheep and watching their children go without - more should've stolen. Should be ten, twenty of them hanging outside the gates.

But there's not.

FRANZ: Cos this town has you, my faithful executioner. Present boldness aside.

JACOB: No sir.

FRANZ: Still schooling me.

JACOB: No sir.

Just, I know why they're calm sir.

A moment.

FRANZ: Well?

JACOB: As is known, herdsmen've always come to the executioner for healing. Take bodies apart enough, you soon learn how to put them back together.

Grandfather, Father, me, came to them, come to me, but at night. Secretly.

But these last months it's different.

See, I've gone to them. Right into their tents.

FRANZ: When?

JACOB: This whole winter.

Going tonight in fact.

I'll tend their wounds. Cool their fevers. Calm them.

Many more should've hanged.

But they didn't.

Cos I healed instead.

A moment.

I want to keep to that.

FRANZ: You have my blessing

JACOB: Only that.

FRANZ: Healer?

JACOB: Will keep them calm.

FRANZ: I need an executioner. Soon one of them'll start up. You'll be needed on the gallows.

JACOB: That's another body rotting and more death in the air, right into your tooth.

FRANZ: You want to be a healer.

JACOB: When Grandfather came to this, times were bad, just like now, cold and hunger, and he stole, was caught, faced the noose, but was given a choice. Either the gallows or he could hang another, executioner being dead -

FRANZ: Know this -

JACOB: And he took the choice to hang another and lived under that shadow. As did my father, and myself. Grandfather and Father, they worked hard for the law. And I've worked hard for it as well. I've kept the law and the law is kept. Even now.

FRANZ: What if a herdsman needs hanging?

JACOB: If one's killed, a hungry one, now... they won't let me in their tents ever again... and I won't catch their sickness and the sicker they get, the angrier they get, and so they steal. I kill them and so they riot and I kill them more and they are still sick and the wheel keeps turning, there's no calm, more and more rot.

But.

If you let me heal -

Can't banish hunger or cold, but I can cure a fever.

Sir, you'll not have a black tooth again!

FRANZ: Haggling, this is haggling.

Jacob. Trader of roles.

So I make you healer. Fine. But it's not just herdsmen get sick. Us inside the walls won't come to you. We'd never come to you.

JACOB: You have.

FRANZ: And no one inside'll ever know.

JACOB: Hals. He came to me.

FRANZ: Don't lie.

JACOB: I don't. He had to. Who else knows how to unpick a body better than me? He had to come. Was his wife. She breathed like she'd a stone on her chest.

FRANZ: The lady Ana walks about, talks loudly, up to her neck in these walls. No sickness on her.

JACOB: Because I lifted it from her.

He came at night. This winter. To my house.

She was under our roof til the sickness left her.

Think of all the souls bound to his happiness. I saved all that.

Have spent far more time healing than taking heads.

This will make things better sir, am sure of it.

If the herdsmen stay calm they'll work harder. The merchants'll double their coin.

Franz *thinks for a bit.*

FRANZ: Who'll take heads?

JACOB: No one.

FRANZ: Must be someone.

JACOB: Taking heads, hanging - town needs all the herdsmen it can get.

FRANZ: And if there's killing and stealing and riot?

JACOB: Can't take all their heads.

No one to work for the merchants.

FRANZ: You want this?

JACOB: Long, long time.

A moment.

FRANZ: Quite an offer.

Will think on it.

But first I'll see about this salt.

Outside a house beyond the the walls, the woods a way off, but visible.

Evening.

Hilde *enters with a bucket and a stick with a hook at one end, fashioned to fit her just so.*

She puts the bucket down.

She uses the hook to pick up chicken bits from the bucket and chuck them on the ground.

HILDE: Ready if you want it!

She keeps scattering chicken bits.

Jacob *enters and creeps up on her quietly.*

She finishes scattering the chicken.

She sees him. She yelps.

JACOB: That for?

HILDE: Crept up on me like some wolf.

JACOB: Only wicked wolf that's here is me.

Who you give them?

HILDE: Gerty.

No eggs for a month. No wings flapping or beak pecking when I picked her up. Knew it was her time.

JACOB: A faithful chicken to the end.

HILDE: Slopped her guts out, put them with the rest. I do right?

What?

JACOB: Look at you, like you were born out here.

HILDE: I'm learning.

JACOB: No, you've learnt. You're a proper outsider now.

HILDE: Not so sure about that, I'm used to the sound of wheels on mud. Heard them on the wind earlier. Howls picked up my hair.

Jacob *tuts.*

Don't cluck at me like that! It's easy for you, you've heard them all your life!

JACOB: Never once hurt those that feed them.

HILDE: These're wolves, not chubby puppies.

JACOB: When Grandfather was a boy there was a herdsman sat round the fire when a wolf came to the light.

HILDE: Gather round children, Grandfather Jacob's telling another tale.

JACOB: This one's a goodun.

HILDE: On with it, Grandpa!

JACOB: So, this wolf, it came to this herdsman, crept through the shadows into the glow of the flames. Had a clean cut down the centre of its face and a wound in its side. Sweet as any pup looking for warmth. So he took pity on it, gave it a piece of meat roasting on the fire. And that wolf stayed with him and he fed it every day. Whatever he had to give, he would. And it even chased packs that came hunting, all the way back to the trees. But when that man died no one fed it anymore and after a time it turned savage, ripped a sheep and ran back to the woods. So us outside've fed them ever since.

Well?

HILDE: It's a good story.

JACOB: A true story.

HILDE: Here's something I know's true. This morning a pack of them stood on the ridge, right over there, staring at the walls.

JACOB: They ever take a chicken of ours?

HILDE: No.

JACOB: Nothing to be scared of then.

HILDE: Am not scared of wolves. Just seeing them more. See this?

She shows him the stick.

He takes it.

He admires her tool.

JACOB: Clever.

HILDE: Wanted a hook for the bucket and a bit of meat. No bending down. And then it came, a waking dream. But I'll have to make another.

Feel it.

Too soft. And the hook's not right. Get it right next time. Pick up any bucket or cloth or bit of meat and never bend down again. Go wherever I please, carry whatever I want. No one ever say I'm workshy again.

JACOB: I've never said so.

HILDE: Cos you're not other people. You're better'n them in that town.

New things I made!

JACOB: I've something new.

HILDE: What?

JACOB: I asked him.

HILDE: Franz?

JACOB: Today.

HILDE: No!

How?

When?

JACOB: Came in and he was bent double with a rotten tooth.

HILDE: How rotten?

JACOB: Black and grey and weeping.

HILDE: Hallelujah.

JACOB: Saw my chance and pounced!

"Can heal your tooth sir, maybe you'll let me heal forever."

HILDE: Clever and bold.

Oh Jacob!

We're going to take one of the walls down.

JACOB: Are we?

HILDE: One on the left where there's no window. Come down easily enough. Build out a little more to the side.

JACOB: Will cost.

HILDE: I'll do it.

JACOB: Not get workmen?

HILDE: Did the path didn't I? Made the bricks, laid them out.

JACOB: A new wall?

HILDE: You'll help.

JACOB: But why?

HILDE: For a child. What else?

JACOB: He's still thinking on it.

HILDE: You said -

JACOB: Give it a week.

HILDE: Been married a year!

JACOB: Then what's a week?

HILDE: Fed up with you pulling your cock out and shooting all over my belly like you've emptied a tub of eels on me.

JACOB: Hilde!

HILDE: Look. Look at our house.

She makes him see it.

The chickens. There, look at them clucking away... Fidget, Bump, Bet, Beak.

A cockerel crows.

And Dick.

JACOB: Stupid name.

HILDE: We've a roof. Four walls. Chickens. Enough land for two or three or four even. And love. So much can grow out of all that.

JACOB: All in the shadow of those walls. See the guards leaning over the parapet, see, look, that one there!

HILDE: We're far from it.

JACOB: A short hop.

HILDE: And that's all it takes to be out from it. There's no walls on either side of us. Our mud's from the earth, not the turning of wheels. Might as well be a whole different country. Never've had all this when I was inside the walls, working for the fucking Justice, scrubbing his floors, tripping down narrow streets and bending down all day so my legs hurt so much and not so much as a hook to let me actually lift, just hard stone steps and angry looks and 'hurry up girl, work faster, no time for laggards like you and this pain of yours that no one sees but you say is there, you're lying, you're lazy, you lying lazy girl, out with you!'

But none of that here!

Here I've tools I've made for me. We've a house we've made together for both of us.

No prying eyes. No cross words. Our own little place. And the time to live in it, to spread out and wait if I need to. Plenty of room for a child here.

He looks at it all.

JACOB: If he says no, then it's under my shadow, and it'll never be new for a child, no matter how lovely it looks.

HILDE: Then why'd'you ask him?

You're thinking different. You're seeing different.

It'll happen.

She goes to kiss him.

She stops herself.

Have you cleaned yourself?

It's dark now, the sun has almost set.

Won't have to think of that soon. You'll be clean. New life.

He draws a knife.

Jacob?

He puts his finger to his lips.

JACOB: Someone's coming.

Someone wearing a hood enters.

The figure takes their hood off.

*It's **Ana**. She has a bundle with her.*

She sees the knife.

ANA: It's me.

Jacob *puts it away.*

She puts her bundle down, grimacing in pain as she does so.

Well it's almost hot, isn't it? Soon be wishing it was the dead of winter again.

She steps in some chicken.

What's this?

HILDE: Chicken.

ANA: On the floor?

HILDE: She's for the wolves.

ANA: Oh?

JACOB: Feed them and they never take a thing.

ANA: Clever!

Husband would never give them one of his sheep.

Though... give the wolves sheep but not his herdsmen? Fits his nature.

JACOB: You know Hals better than us madam.

ANA: Have said to call me Ana.

Shame you put it on the floor. So hungry could eat a turkey.

Comes from the other side of the world, a big bird with a wobbly chin, looks magnificent on a plate. Though the shame of it is they're dry as bone.

Father had some for his table when he was still in coin. Felt sorry for them when I saw them caged, then I got close and one bit me on the nose. Made sure I saw him slaughtered and ate his leg with relish.

JACOB: You doing here madam? Forgive me, but it's not often fine-clothed figures pass through the gates at dusk. Specially not the wife of one so high in the walls.

ANA: Husband's away. Not a soul saw me.

HILDE: What's that?

ANA: Take a look.

> **Hilde** *grabs her stick and opens it.*
>
> *In it is a book and a knife.*
>
> **Ana** *bends down and hands them to her.*
>
> **Hilde** *admires it.*

Saw all the things you've made, thought this might help you make more.

HILDE: Thank you.

ANA: No, thank you. Was you pulled the fever from my throat.

HILDE: That was husband.

ANA: You let me into your home. There's never enough thanks for that.

> **Ana** *hands him the book, he won't take it.*

Take it.

JACOB: Have brought us two already.

ANA: Then have a third.

JACOB: He'll see a third.

ANA: He won't.

HILDE: Certain?

ANA: Books're for his walls. Make Franz the Justice and other big men mad with envy. But what's the point of a thousand books if you never look inside them and take in their beauty?

Ever wanted to gaze at the sea? I grew up next to it. This book takes you there. You'll peer off the edge of the world.

HILDE: Take it.

JACOB: Two was thanks enough.

HILDE: I'm keeping the knife.

> **Ana** *shakes her head.*
>
> *She bends down to put the book back.*
>
> *She winces.*

The matter?

ANA: My side.

> **Ana** *lifts.*
>
> *She is bruised.*
>
> **Hilde** *sees now, goes over, looks.*

HILDE: How'd it happen?

ANA: Did it myself.

HILDE: Not Hals?

ANA: To myself.

HILDE: I know Hals.

JACOB: Hilde.

HILDE: She comes in secret, a blue bruise down her side, she should say.

ANA: It was me.

HILDE: Fine, but who'll pay. Husband's to be healer now -

JACOB: Hilde -

HILDE: We need a fee. A good fee.

ANA: Healer? When?

HILDE: Soon.

ANA: I can bring more books, another knife. Hals can't know.

HILDE: Why? Secrets cost more.

ANA: When I first came here… had never seen the herdsmen up close before.

I have begged and begged him to feed them.

But he won't.

So this morning, when he went away, I went to his cellar. Stood on a ladder and reached up for a sack of grain, so high he'd never notice, but slipped, landed on my side.

JACOB: Know who I am?

ANA: You're Jacob.

Am not asking you to help, just to heal my side.

JACOB: It's theft.

ANA: The herdsmen are starving.

A moment.

HILDE: I want another book. And I'd like another knife.

ANA: You'll have it.

HILDE: I'll get the cloth.

Hilde *exits.*

ANA: Thank you.

Hilde *reenters with a book and cloth.*

JACOB: Lift it up.

Hilde *does.*

Jacob *spits on his hands.*

ANA: I've told you not to with me.

JACOB: Not clean.

ANA: Believe that? I don't.

JACOB: Town does.

ANA: I'm not from town.

JACOB: Christ cleaned himself this way.

ANA: You're not Christ.

JACOB: Town demands. I oblige.

ANA: Just cos the word's're old, doesn't mean you've to follow them.

> **Jacob** *spits on his hands, rubs them together.*
>
> *He examines her.*
>
> Is it bad?
>
> *He touches her.*
>
> *She winces.*

JACOB: Turn this way.

> *She does.*
>
> *He nods.*
>
> *He gestures for her to put her clothes down.*
>
> Just a bruise.
>
> Will wrap it.
>
> It'll hurt.
>
> **Ana** *nods.*
>
> *He wraps her side.*
>
> *It does hurt, but he is quick and skilful.*
>
> Better?
>
> *She moves about.*

ANA: Yes.

> Thank you.

JACOB: Take you to the gate?

ANA: No need.

JACOB: It's not safe to pass through the herdsmen's tents.

ANA: Just brought them food.

Little bit of trust, that's all that's needed.

She hands **Hilde** *the book.*

Hilde, I hope you make so much with that blade.

HILDE: Make more with two.

ANA: Yes, of course.

Thank you, both of you.

She puts her hood up and goes.

HILDE: She scares me.

Think she'll keep feeding them?

JACOB: Hope not. She keeps stealing and Hals'll find out. Then she'll be in the cells. Or whipped in the square.

HILDE: You'll be healer then.

JACOB: Who else'll do it?

HILDE: Hals won't accept her being whipped. One so high, his wife, whipped? No.

JACOB: Franz can't know. Me helping her, covering her, taking Hals' book.

HILDE: When you're healer, they'll all come. Just you wait. Her, Hals, the Justice, right to you. Already have.

We going to the herdsmen tonight?

JACOB: Course.

HILDE: Am tired of going at night.

JACOB: Me too.

HILDE: Soon you'll be healing in the day and I'll be here whittling, building, working.

JACOB: Won't keep with me?

HILDE: No. Herdsmen look at you funny, look at me funny.

Can't forgive them that.

JACOB: Hilde.

HILDE: Will be neighbour if they're neighbour to me.

JACOB: See if Franz says yes first.

HILDE: He'll say yes.

JACOB: So certain.

*

A few days later.

Night.

Inside **Hilde** *and* **Jacob's** *house.*

Hilde *is reading the Bible - sometimes she falters but she reads clearly.*

HILDE: And there shall come forth a rod out of the stem of Jesse.

And the spirit of the LORD shall rest upon him.

And with righteousness shall he judge the poor.

And on that day the wolf shall dwell with the lamb, and the leopard shall lie down with the kid; and the lion shall eat straw like the ox.

She breaks off.

Like an ox? Eat straw like an ox?

JACOB: What it says.

HILDE: But what's it mean?

JACOB: That all will be well.

HILDE: When?

JACOB: When Christ returns.

HILDE: And when's that?

JACOB: Doesn't say.

HILDE: Well I'm tired of waiting, I'm going to make it new, whether he's coming tomorrow or in a thousand years.

She looks at the book.

The lion shall eat straw...you'd struggle to make a lion eat straw.

He laughs.

JACOB: You read beautifully.

HILDE: You teach beautifully.

Now enough of this, read me a story.

He goes to a book.

From the new book.

JACOB: Hilde.

HILDE: It's been sat there long enough. A good book like that for a few scraps of cloth. A sin to leave it there.

He picks up **Ana's** *book.*

JACOB: Should give it back.

HILDE: It was payment.

JACOB: Stolen.

HILDE: And you want to read it. And I want you to read it. Stop acting otherwise.

They snuggle up.

He opens the book.

JACOB: Once upon a time there was a certain merchant who possessed wealth and cattle, and had a wife and children; and God, whose name be exalted, had also endowed him with the knowledge of the languages of beasts and birds. The abode of this merchant -

Hilde *shifts her weight, makes a sound of pain.*

My love?

HILDE: Been up and about all day. Knew it'd start tonight.

He gets up, holds her feet, massages them.

Hate them.

JACOB: I love them. Stronger than any legs in those walls.

He kisses her feet.

Smelly though.

She hits him.

HILDE: Stupid man!

JACOB: Love all of you.

HILDE: Love all of you.

Don't stop.

He massages her feet for a bit.

She sits up.

Hear that?

They listen.

Wolves on the wind.

The noise gets louder and louder and louder.

Suddenly, it stops.

HILDE: Sounded close.

JACOB: Sometimes they're close, sometimes they're not.

HILDE: Herdsman told me tonight he'd seen them moving down the ridge the other night.

JACOB: When?

HILDE: You were with his child.

Thought Franz said soon.

JACOB: He did.

HILDE: Remind him.

JACOB: In a bit.

HILDE: Want us here when sun's down, not crouching in a tent, getting home cold and tired.

Want more time to read and hold you.

JACOB: We keep doing as well much as we can, then he'll see. He'll have to make me healer.

HILDE: Make him see. Tell him. Show him. Demand.

JACOB: Do this work, he will!

HILDE: He's a merchant.

Go to him straight.

Make him an offer.

Make him!

JACOB: Alright!

I'll press.

HILDE: When?

JACOB: Tomorrow!

Now shush.

She snuggles up once more.

The abode of this merchant was in the country; and he had, in his house, an ass and a bull. When the bull came to the place where the ass was tied, he found it swept and sprinkled and the ass was lying at his ease and it happened, one day, that the merchant overheard the bull saying to the ass, 'May thy food benefit thee! I am oppressed with fatigue, while thou art enjoying repose: you eat sifted barley, and men serve you; and it is only occasionally that thy master rides thee, and returns; while I am continually employed in ploughing, and turning the mill.'

There are cries in the distance, wolves and people.

Hilde *and* **Jacob** *spring up.*

JACOB: Too close.

Should I go?

HILDE: Go?

There's a shout from outside.

Jacob *draws a knife.*

There's a banging on the door.

He approaches it, opens.

Wilf, *falls through the open doorway.*

Jacob *catches him.*

Wilf's *leg is covered in blood.*

Jacob *lays him on the ground.*

JACOB: Water!

Hilde *sees, she gets a bucket of water.*

Jacob *splashes water on* **Wilf's** *leg.*

Wilf *sits up, sees* **Jacob**, *sees who he is.*

WILF: God.

Oh God.

God, don't -

Please, had to, please.

He tries to wriggle free.

JACOB: Keep still.

He tries to help **Wilf**.

Wilf *backs away.*

WILF: Please, please, beg you.

JACOB: Look -

WILF: Sorry sorry.

JACOB: Who are you?

WILF: The lookout.

JACOB: Happened?

WILF: Didn't mean - their teeth - slobbering, spitting fire. Shouted to the tents, flashed the torch, ran, one got me.

Must know I never -

He tries to rise.

His leg buckles underneath him.

Christ.

Jacob *offers his hand.*

Wilf *won't take it.*

Jacob *shakes his head, goes to get his sword off the wall.*

JACOB: Knife Ana give you near at hand?

HILDE: You're not going.

JACOB: Be safe with this.

HILDE: Look at him.

JACOB: How many're out there?

Speak!

WILF: Too many.

HILDE: Stay.

JACOB: Hold that knife close. Anything comes through the door you stick it in the gut.

HILDE: Coming with you.

JACOB: You're not.

HILDE: Can fight!

JACOB: He needs tending.

HILDE: Think the herdsmen'd help us?

All we've done for them this winter and this one still won't touch you!

Jacob *ignores her.*

She grabs him.

You're a man of flesh and bone. Remember that.

He kisses her.

He leaves.

A moment.

She looks at the door.

She looks at **Wilf.**

She makes a decision, picks up her knife and marches to the door.

The wolves are howling, people shout and scream.

She sees all this, hears all this, takes all this in.

Wilf *crawls over and grabs her leg.*

WILF: Please.

She looks at **Wilf**.

She closes the door.

*

Next morning.

Hilde *is sitting next to* **Wilf**.

He wakes.

She reaches to touch his forehead, he avoids her.

HILDE: Seeing if you've a fever.

She reaches out again, he dodges her.

WILF: You clean?

HILDE: Are you?

WILF: I -

HILDE: You were lookout, supposed to raise the alarm. But you didn't.

WILF: Did.

HILDE: Not in time.

How many've died cos of you?

But it's me who's unclean?

He doesn't answer.

She washes her hand with water.

WILF: Thought with spit.

HILDE: Spit's for the executioner, after he's been in the cells, on the gallows.

Water's for us all.

Now let me see cos I'm not washing any other part of me.

She puts a hand to his head.

You're not feverish.

She gets water.

Drink this.

He hesitates.

Drew it from the well myself!

He sniffs the water, sips.

WILF: Sweet.

HILDE: Good. Sugar should hide the poison.

A while.

WILF: Will it get better?

HILDE: Husband could say.

WILF: Can't you?

Seen you with him.

Must know something.

HILDE: You'll live.

A while.

WILF: Think they're dead?

HILDE: Who?

A while.

WILF: Should die.

HILDE: Pissed off if you do, your body stiff in my bed.

WILF: A one-legged lookout, what's the good of that?

HILDE: Oh pity, pity you!

See these?

She points at her legs.

Sometimes these hurt. And my back. And my side. Hurt, hurt all over. But you've got to let it hurt. And it goes. Or you touch it and it heals.

Like this. Hold still.

She takes his bandages and undoes them.

She takes cloth and cleans it.

She changes the dressing.

Better?

WILF: Bit.

She picks up her stick.

HILDE: This is for picking up.

Have hooks for hanging and put them on the wall, just so, for me. No bending or stretching.

I boil my pots when they're dirty so I don't bend down and scrub.

There's a way to live well if you're canny.

And anyway, you don't need two legs to keep watch, just need to stand and not fucking run.

WILF: You're clever.

HILDE: What's your name?

WILF: Wilf.

HILDE: Hilde.

How many were there?

And be honest.

WILF: Wasn't a pack.

Was all of them.

Far too many.

Angry. Hunger makes you that.

Seen them outside the trees these last few weeks. Heard them too. At odd times.

Always to happen.

Take revenge.

HILDE: For what? Should be us tearing them up.

WILF: So walled in.

HILDE: So what?

WILF: Walled in.

HILDE: Me?

WILF: Weren't born out here were you?

You'd know otherwise. You'd see it. Smell it.

HILDE: Know what?

WILF: Woods came all the way here once. Then trees were chopped, walls built, tents up and we started living under cloth.

Wolves were always coming back. Take what should be theirs.

A knock.

Hilde *goes to the door.*

It's **Franz.**

He has a bandage round his head.

FRANZ: Where is he?

HILDE: Haven't seen him?

FRANZ: He's alive.

Just looking for him.

She tries to hold back her relief.

That?

Wilf *tries to stand and bow but falls down.*

HILDE: Wolf got him.

Franz *points at* **Wilf's** *leg*

FRANZ: Husband's work?

HILDE: Yes.

Franz *examines* **Wilf**.

Your tooth sir?

FRANZ: Of it?

HILDE: Husband helped you with it?

FRANZ: Hush!

HILDE: Not a soul knows.

FRANZ: Apart from you.

HILDE: Am his wife. Will never tell.

It helping?

FRANZ: Yes.

So, he a herdsman?

WILF: Sir.

Jacob *enters.*

Hilde *rushes to him.*

Franz *gives them a moment.*

JACOB: Sir?

FRANZ: Well done.

JACOB: For what?

FRANZ: Was on the walls, saw everything.

JACOB: Not just me.

HILDE: Take the praise.

FRANZ: Looked like the end of time itself. The woods emptying themselves on the walls.

JACOB: Herdsmen say it's judgement for town chopping down the trees.

WILF: Is.

They stare at **Wilf**.

FRANZ: What's your view?

JACOB: Hungry enough, cold enough, wouldn't you band together and take what you could?

A moment.

Forgive me sir, but why you here?

FRANZ: How many dead?

JACOB: Need another graveyard I reckon.

WILF: God forgive me.

FRANZ: I'm speaking of sheep.

How many?

JACOB: Merchants haven't counted their stock?

FRANZ: Won't leave the walls.

Tried to take a look myself, but there's murder in the herdsmen's eyes.

My guard thought it best I leave.

So I came to you.

Well?

JACOB: Come spring there'll be lambs.

FRANZ: That bad?

Even if each ewe pushes out a pair, it'll be years until we've as many.

And if there's another winter like this one -

It was all sewn up.

Spring on the way, warm days coming.

God I'm tired.

Two merchants went out with swords. See them?

JACOB: No.

FRANZ: Both died. One had his guts ripped out.

JACOB: Bad way to die.

FRANZ: Worse is the merchants saw.

Hals' saw.

They're angry and they want a head.

Who would you choose?

Jacob *doesn't answer.*

Must be a name.

JACOB: Has taken me months to win just a bit of trust from them.

FRANZ: I don't like it either.

JACOB: Be no peace if one's taken

FRANZ: Sure?

JACOB: After last night, yes.

FRANZ: What's one head?

JACOB: Everything.

FRANZ: Just need one.

A moment.

Jacob *turns to* **Hilde**.

He turns to **Franz**.

JACOB: Him.

WILF: No.

HILDE: Jacob.

JACOB: He was lookout.

Let them through.

FRANZ: Hiding him?

WILF: Far too many.

JACOB: Quiet.

He came. I sheltered him. Went to help the herdsmen.

FRANZ: Merchants'll accept him.

WILF: Please.

JACOB: Shut up!

Will, yes, merchants will, but the herdsmen won't.

He's a stupid boy, but he's their stupid boy.

Aren't you?

Aren't you their stupid boy?

A moment.

HILDE: Wilf?

Are you their stupid boy?

WILF: Yes.

Am.

FRANZ: Two merchants dead cos of him!

JACOB: Have taken heads for theft and killing. But for error?

FRANZ: Hals calls for a head, the other merchants follow.

JACOB: How're the herdsmen boy?

HILDE: Wilf.

JACOB: How are they Wilf?

WILF: Starving.

JACOB: Angry?

WILF: Yes.

JACOB: Sick?

WILF: Less since you and her started to heal.

JACOB: Do they plot?

Answer.

WILF: Some want to take sheep. Skin them. Cook them.

Others to slip through the gates and steal.

Some to leave.

JACOB: See?

Herdsmen see him living, walking, breathing, they see mercy.

And that will calm them.

They will stay.

And I can keep healing.

And then they're even calmer.

And this town rebuilds.

FRANZ: But if they revolt?

JACOB: Then his head'll be above the gate.

And serves them right.

For now he stands as a sign of what is to come. A clean wound for those who live. A better life. And a warning.

This settles.

FRANZ: Will tell Hals.

HILDE: He'll listen?

FRANZ: Others will follow if he does.

HILDE: Tell him if his workers're happy, in time his coin'll double.

FRANZ: How you'd offer it is it? Tell him every merchant's hope, double of everything forever.

JACOB: Forgive her sir.

FRANZ: Will talk to Hals.

You keep your sword on the wall.

But keep it sharp.

He makes to go.

HILDE: Is he healer?

FRANZ: Lord you're bold, always were, even when you scrubbed my floor, when you weren't leaning back, doing nothing.

HILDE: Is he healer?

FRANZ: For now.

Yes.

Though my tooth still hurts.

JACOB: Keep with the salt sir.

FRANZ: Have rubbed it twice a day.

JACOB: Keep with it.

Franz *leaves.*

Wilf *stares at him.*

You feverish?

Jacob *touches* **Wilf's** *head.*

Wilf *freezes.*

You've worked a miracle.

Jacob *examines* **Wilf's** *bandages*

I'll take you to the tents.

HILDE: Let me.

JACOB: Needed there, start my work.

Come on, put your arm over my shoulder.

Hilde: Wait.

Hilde *gives her stick, gives it to* **Wilf**.

Better with this.

Wilf: It's yours.

Hilde: Keep it.

Wilf *struggles to his feet.*

Put it under your arm.

He does.

That's it.

He moves, hopping.

Good.

Now hop outside.

Wilf *goes outside, leaning on the stick.*

The two of them wait for a bit.

You gambled Wilf's life.

JACOB: Oh stop, you pinned the Justice down.

HILDE: Not the same as staking a life on yours.

JACOB: Else should I've done?

I did right.

You know I did.

Only way to save his head.

HILDE: You're healer.

JACOB: And you got Franz to say it!

I'm not executioner anymore.

It's happening.

The wolf lying down with the lamb.

HILDE: This is not God Jacob.

JACOB: No, but, what is it then?

HILDE: That was reading Jacob.

JACOB: Well what is this all then?

HILDE: It's the world moving over.

And it could roll back just as easy.

You've got to make it stick.

JACOB: I will.

HILDE: Talk's not enough. Hope's not enough.

He touches her arm, leans into her.

JACOB: My love.

We have it.

HILDE: They're waiting for you.

*

Outside the wall, near the tents.

Jacob *and* **Wilf** *enter.*

Wilf *stops.*

He's taking it in.

Jacob *lets him wait.*

Jacob: Just a few more steps.

Wilf *still doesn't move.*

WILF: Does it go?

JACOB: Gets smaller. Over time.

That'll need seeing to, come back in two days.

WILF: She helped me. Not you.

JACOB: Will help if you need it.

WILF: Justice says you're healer, doesn't mean I see you as that.

JACOB: Even though he's said?

WILF: You've come to our tents, yes, but you're always executioner.

JACOB: Can help.

WILF: Help get my leg back?

Help birth a thousand sheep?

Make the starved fat?

How many of us've you killed?

Kill me if we don't go with you.

JACOB: Then make them!

WILF: How? We hate you.

My head'll be up there in a week!

JACOB: You've to keep them sweet.

WILF: For you? No.

JACOB: Show them your leg. Show them my work.

WILF: Wife's work.

JACOB: Tell them it's mine.

Tell them I sheltered you.

That I spoke for you.

That I will come to them under the light of the sun and make them whole.

WILF: You're no Christ, executioner. Be speaking for the devil.

JACOB: No, speaking for yourself.

WILF: Last night was lookout.

Back to the wall, face to the trees.

A man. Facing black night and the woods.

A torch.

A watcher.

And now, speaking for you.

JACOB: You're a messenger Wilf.

You speak for me and I do my work, there'll never be a head or a body or a limb hanging from town's ramparts ever again.

WILF: Big promise that.

Wilf *moves off.*

JACOB: Help you to the tents.

WILF: Better myself.

Shows this leg's fixed.

Won't say it was her.

Will say it was all you, wonderful you.

JACOB: But Wilf -

WILF: What?

JACOB: Who should I go to first?

WILF: The sickest.

JACOB: Who has height in the tents?

WILF: Who am I messenger to then? My lot, or you?

JACOB: Both.

WILF: We don't have height, we're not town.

JACOB: Must be a big man.

WILF: Lived out here all your life, but still so walled in.

JACOB: Tell me.

WILF: We have big men and big women.

Go to the tent in the middle.

See how they are.

Word spreads from them.

I'll go now, tell them you're coming.

Will start there and walk through those who live.

Will take days, weeks.

JACOB: Come find me, tell me what they say.

*Wilf starts to leave. Then **Ana** enters.*

She has a basket of bread.

*She offers some food to **Wilf**. He takes some.*

ANA: Who was that?

JACOB: Wilf. Sheltered with us.

She offers him bread, he shakes his head.

ANA: Take it.

JACOB: It's from your husband's cellar.

ANA: Hals won't see. He's taken to drink. Been a hard day for him. Passed out in a puddle of piss.

JACOB: Guards on the walls can see you.

ANA: Let them.

They've cellars full of food.

JACOB: Going to steal from them as well?

ANA: I just might.

JACOB: Don't joke.

ANA: I don't.

My husband and his merchant friends want to sleep sound in their beds, they'd better feed their herdsmen, or their throats'll run red and right that would be too!

I'll take their gold if needs be.

JACOB: You'll be in the cells.

ANA: Will not. There's no executioner.

Franz stood at the gates. The whole town knows.

JACOB: Get back in the walls.

ANA: Not til I've given everything in this basket.

JACOB: You keep at this and you'll be in a cell, and I'll be back taking heads by next sabbath.

Be clever.

ANA: This isn't a time for clever.

JACOB: Catch you out here with bread again, will march you straight to Hals.

ANA: Oh Jacob, we both know you'll do no such thing.

Am going to keep being stupid.

JACOB: Please go inside.

ANA: I can help you.

JACOB: How?

ANA: How? I'm Hals' wife. I see and I hear them, all the merchants, scurrying and planning and thinking.

I can tell you what they know.

I can tell you if they think it's working. All this.

I will keep you healer.

A moment.

JACOB: Why?

ANA: Was brought here on a cart by Hals.

Will do anything to help those he owns.

A moment.

Why you standing here? Go.

*

A few days later.

Evening.

*Inside **Hilde** and **Jacob's** house.*

***Hilde** dunks two bits of cloth into a bucket of water.*

She takes the bits of cloth out of the bucket.

She drops them on the floor.

She puts one foot over each cloth.

She starts skating across the floor.

She makes swooshing noises.

She exaggerates her arms.

She is skating and cleaning.

***Wilf** enters. He moves with much greater ease now. He has **Hilde's** stick from before with him.*

***Hilde** has her back to him, doesn't see him.*

He stays close to the door, watching her.

She turns, sees him, stops.

WILF: Doing?

HILDE: Cleaning.

WILF: Doesn't look it.

HILDE: Well it is.

WILF: Have to bend down.

HILDE: Says who?

WILF: Everyone.

HILDE: I don't bend to clean.

WILF: Why?

HILDE: Hurts me.

Clean like this.

WILF: Looks like skating.

HILDE: Not looks like, is.

WILF: Then it's skating not cleaning.

HILDE: Well, always liked skating.

Every day a holiday.

WILF: Never skated.

Just watched you walled ins have your fun.

Cleaned lots of floors?

HILDE: Cleaned the Justice's floors.

WILF: He let you clean like this?

HILDE: Saw me once, shouted. Often shouted. Too slow. Or too lazy. Or too lying, lying I hurt so much.

Much better out here.

How's your leg?

40

WILF: Better this week.

Here.

He offers the stick.

Can walk without it now.

She takes it.

HILDE: Jacob'll want a look.

Seen him?

WILF: Doing his rounds.

Gave the head man a new shepherd's crook.

HILDE: He take it?

WILF: Didn't want to touch it at first.

HILDE: I made that.

WILF: Should be you who gave it then.

HILDE: Is a good man.

WILF: Wants to be. Shines out his face.

HILDE: You come here just to insult? Cos you're standing in his house, my house, came through his door willingly, took his healing -

WILF: Your healing -

HILDE: He's the one I learned from.

Give him time.

Let it run.

WILF: Have to don't I?

It fails and my head's outside the gates.

HILDE: Is it failing?

WILF: Head man did take the crook.

Had to speak to him, tell him to take, but he did.

Speak like that every waking moment.

Then tell him, your husband, what they're saying, who to go to next.

Have started to get sharp looks.

What am I?

HILDE: You're a Wilf. A very good Wilf.

WILF: Am messenger.

What your husband called me.

To my people.

Used to stand, used to be ready to fight.

But I ran.

And my leg.

There's a bit missing.

Can't be a talker.

Was Wilf the lookout.

Now I find sick people for him.

Bring him to them, them to him.

Tell them that he's here to help.

Soothe their fears.

HILDE: Do they listen?

WILF: Do.

HILDE: So bad about that?

WILF: Not pick up a sheep on its back. Not pull out a lamb. Not swing it if there's no breath. Not patch a canvas. Not fight with wolves. Not walk the sheep to pasture. Can't use this body for that. What am I?

A moment.

She dunks some cloths in the bucket, throws them on the ground.

HILDE: Here.

He comes further in, puts his feet over the wet cloth.

He starts skating. It is slow and painful for him, but he does it.

That's it.

She joins him.

They skate.

They laugh.

Keep skating.

He does.

Jacob *enters.*

Wilf *stops.*

HILDE: Look who's visiting.

How's today?

JACOB: Not a soul asked me to clean myself.

HILDE: No one?

JACOB: First time.

WILF: Head man shook his hand.

No washing afterwards.

HILDE: It's working.

JACOB: Thank you Wilf.

WILF: Thanks?

JACOB: For your words. To them. Your people.

WILF: Doing it for my head.

Remember?

JACOB: Thanks nevertheless.

Ana *bursts in.*

HILDE: Easy with the door!

ANA: Sorry.

JACOB: You sneak out as loudly as this?

ANA: I've a thought to share. It's brilliant. Glitters!

Who're you?

WILF: Wilf.

JACOB: Do you have news of inside?

ANA: Listen to my thought first.

HILDE: Tell him what you know.

ANA: Thought first.

JACOB: On with it.

ANA: Everyone should get when they need.

A moment.

HILDE: And what's that?

ANA: Should be a basket of food next to Jacob when he works. A bandage for a babe, a sausage for its father. Some ointment for one, a pie for another.

HILDE: The things in your head.

ANA: You dream of tools, I dream of that.

JACOB: What's food to do with healing?

ANA: Can't get better with an empty belly.

HILDE: You can't carve grain like a piece of wood.

ANA: Can when you've mountains of it like I do.

JACOB: All in cellars. None of it yours.

ANA: It's not anyone's if it stays uneaten. The sheep're dead. Who's it for?

JACOB: So I heal and you hand out stolen grain? No.

ANA: They'll get sicker and sicker no matter what you do.

WILF: They are getting better.

ANA: Who are you?

WILF: Wilf.

Lookout.

We're not starving just yet.

ANA: But you were.

Lot of you are dead, food'll run out soon.

I can give this.

HILDE: They'll be hanged for eating stolen grain.

ANA: Can't just patch up their wounds.

JACOB: Is not patching -

ANA: Have spoken to servants, some wives. They think the same.

JACOB: They do not.

ANA: While all the merchants are muttering in my husband's room, we're to fill a cart and take it out the gates.

JACOB: You won't!

ANA: You'll heal, I'll hand out sausages.

JACOB: Telling me this for?

ANA: Because I've heard the merchants.

HILDE: They said?

ANA: Husband was saying he needs sheep brought from far over, men to go and herd them to the town.

They need herdsmen.

But they're so stupid. So fat and stupid.

They want this to be now, not in months, but now.

Herdsmen won't get better when the food goes, they'll riot, husband will act against them. Lazy. He's calling you lazy Wilf.

They need the Justice, Franz the Justice, to let the light into their cellars, let all that grain out, and they'll have the workers they need. But they can't see that.

HILDE: And you can make them see it?

ANA: No. But Jacob can.

JACOB: How?

ANA: You speak to Franz. You tell him you need the merchants to open their stores -

JACOB: No -

ANA: Fine, fine, then the first plan it is then. I get a cart, load it with food, get caught and you whip me in the square, back taking heads by next sabbath.

JACOB: Some friend you are.

ANA: An extraordinary friend, a good friend.

JACOB: One problem.

See him over there?

I'll have his head in my hands if punishing's my role.

ANA: Liar.

HILDE: This frightens me.

ANA: But they need food.

WILF: Yes lady, but need lots more than that!

A moment.

When Dad's Dad was young, we grew our own.

Fields full of grain, our grain. Our sheep. Ours.

Now we're kept and fed like sheep. One trough for them, another for us.

And this winter, their trough was full, ours empty.

But grain's just a piece of it.

We can't build.

Dad tried. When born he tried.

Town guard came, pulled the house down.

Lots of stories like that.

ANA: I've seen.

WILF: You've not seen til you've lived it.

ANA: Do you need?

WILF: Not a cart. And not stealing.

JACOB: What then?

WILF: She's right, can see it, it's still all new, you healing...when hunger bites...

JACOB: Give it time.

WILF: Want to keep my head.

ANA: Then what do you need?

WILF: Land.

HILDE: This is mad.

ANA: Let him speak.

HILDE: You come through the tents, what, once, twice? You've lived here, what, a year? And you want to save them all, a high lady like you? Rip it all down, this whole world that you know nothing of, and tip me and husband into a river you can't bend.

ANA: I was bought Hilde.

Bought and then dragged here.

To marry a merchant.

So yes I want to save them, save myself, save us all!

And now the walls are down.

The woods emptied themselves.

You want it safe?

You want it in one place?

It never was.

She goes to **Wilf**.

Can get you grain.

WILF: Can you?

ANA: Scatter it over the ground when this winter's done.

HILDE: You know nothing of it.

JACOB: Do you want Wilf safe?

HILDE: Yes.

JACOB: Then I should speak to Franz.

HILDE: Saying she's right?

JACOB: She sees and hears them.

ANA: You must demand, not speak.

HILDE: If he says no?

ANA: He can't.

A moment.

WILF: Please speak to him.

Or it's my head.

He goes to the door.

HILDE: Going?

WILF: To the tents.

Speak to my people. Tell them the news. Land on the way. Keep calm. Messenger aren't I?

ANA: I'll walk with you.

WILF: If you like.

ANA: It's so close.

HILDE: Go.

Wilf *and* **Ana** *leave.*

A moment.

All this cos you offered to fix a tooth.

Can you see Franz saying yes?

JACOB: If he says yes, then we'll have it all.

HILDE: Merchant's don't share.

She's stupid.

JACOB: Think she's right though.

HILDE: Wilf says she is.

If Franz says no and they riot or Ana takes a cart of food and you have to whip her, I will still want you, whoever you are, whatever you do.

Like I want you now.

Now Jacob.

Want you.

JACOB: Want you too.

HILDE: You and me. Warm.

So close to everything we want.

Fuck town.

And I want you.

JACOB: Want you too.

HILDE: You're healer. For now you're healer. Will always be healer to me.

Lie with me.

Keep me warm.

She kisses him and he kisses back and they grab and they fall into one another.

*

Next day.

Inside the walls.

Franz *spits blood into a bowl.*

He groans.

FRANZ: Salt! You said fucking salt!

Look!

He shows the contents of the bowl to **Jacob.**

He puts the bowl aside.

He sits down.

Jacob *approaches* **Franz.**

He puts his hand on his forehead.

JACOB: You've a fever.

Need to pull.

FRANZ: You promised.

JACOB: If you'd let me pull when I first saw you -

FRANZ: And what, leave a great gaping hole?

He spits again.

JACOB: I pull it and straight away put salt in.

FRANZ: Soak it in wine? A few cloves of garlic?

JACOB: Sir.

FRANZ: NO!

He grabs his tooth, he shouts with pain.

He speaks through the agony.

No.

We talk about the herdsmen.

About what you've said.

Your mad words.

Come to me, say they want land, food, crops to grow, build their own houses.

JACOB: Not want. Need.

FRANZ: They want to start trading as well? Perhaps one of them can be Justice.

God!

JACOB: It is so close sir. The peace I promised.

FRANZ: What peace?!

JACOB: This one thing.

FRANZ: No. Not one thing. Is stone, is ploughs, is land deeds. Herdsmen want to own all the land outside the walls.

Not herdsmen then are they?

They're town!

JACOB: They'll riot or they will leave sir.

FRANZ: You or them speaking?

JACOB: Them.

FRANZ: You sold me a promise about peace. Like you sold me a promise about salt.

Well I've to sell your promise to the merchants.

You think it's just a few fine words. A bit of coin dropped in someone's pocket. A promise made. A favour called in. Me flashing my rank at the merchants and they all fall in behind my words.

JACOB: You're the Justice sir.

FRANZ: Ha!

Stupid man!

I'm their Justice.

When I proclaimed you healer and spared that lookout's life, I had them all in here, all the merchants, Hals the biggest of them all, right where you're stood, calling for my blood. My blood. Saying straight to my face that if things start to crumble they'll have the guards out the gates, ripping through the tents, kill every tenth man they find, then hang me from the ramparts.

Hals and his friends.

I've no more credit. They'll have my head. And you'll take it.

JACOB: But sir -

FRANZ: How is it you know so little?

Their coin pays the town guard, pays for me, pays for all this!

Their coin pays for you!

JACOB: You must try.

FRANZ: Why?

JACOB: Cos if they don't listen, herdsmen'll be through the gates or they'll make their way elsewhere. Find another town to serve.

Hals'll come for you.

Franz *laughs.*

FRANZ: Selling to me well Jacob!

Oh God what shall I do?

He leans over, spits, perhaps even sobs a bit.

My tooth stays in.

JACOB: Sir -

FRANZ: Can't speak to Hals with a mouthful of blood.

Pull it afterwards.

Fill the hole with salt.

Put rosemary in as well.

He spits.

There is noise outside.

What's that?

He spits.

Jacob *goes to the window.*

Well?

The noise outside is getting louder and louder.

Franz *joins him.*

Ana *enters.*

FRANZ: The Lady Ana.

ANA: Did you give them to him?

FRANZ: Give who?

ANA: Guards, did you give them to my husband?.

JACOB: Happened?

ANA: Hals has been to the tents. Town guard with him. He's got Wilf.

Did you give them to him?

FRANZ: Give what?

ANA: My husband command of the guard?

FRANZ: Madam, how's it you've been married to your husband a year and know so little of him? Be better off telling the wind to change course.

JACOB: Be riot for sure now.

FRANZ: Do the herdsmen have weapons?

Do they have a wall?

Do they have armoured guards?

Hals and his fellows're quite safe.

JACOB: But later, herdsmen'll get through. Or try to.

FRANZ: I'd wager on the town guard throwing them from the ramparts.

They just want a head Jacob.

And they've chosen this Wilf's. Not mine.

You can heal those that live.

ANA: That's it?!

FRANZ: Would you have me do?

ANA: Cut my husband's throat.

FRANZ: May as well cut mine if I do that.

There is very loud noise outside.

Franz *looks out the window.*

The've just put him in the cells.

We're standing right above him.

ANA: Don't go Jacob.

JACOB: They want him dead, he'll be dead, whether me or no.

ANA: You can choose not to.

JACOB: No you can!

I've no height in these walls. You go out the walls and spread grain like you're feeding birds. Then you go back inside them, safe and are tucked up in fresh sheets. All I have is my conduct and obedience.

ANA: So fucking stupid!

Here's me. Father rose high but he lost it all, took to drink and spending on credit. Then old Hals comes with a sack of coin, an eye for me, and a stench of sheep. Father's lips dripped thinking of what I met fetch.

But even I can choose!

I choose to take his bread and give it to the hungry.

Can't march through time with the law on your lips! You think beyond, you tear down, you move when you can, you see a better city in a better place on the other side of your eyes.

JACOB: Not everyone has new words for new things.

ANA: Hilde does. The things that woman could do if she was left to run wild.

FRANZ: Please leave.

ANA: Oh bless you both.

FRANZ: Good day madam.

ANA: Bless you Jacob.

JACOB: Don't need your blessing.

ANA: Your soul does.

She goes.

FRANZ: I feel light.

JACOB: It's your tooth.

FRANZ: Yes, yes.

JACOB: Haven't got my tools to pull it.

FRANZ: Get to that Wilf downstairs.

Come tomorrow.

Will give me a last night with this fucking tooth.

*

A cell.

Wilf *is tied to a chair. He's been beaten.*

Jacob *enters, unties him.*

JACOB: Do you hurt?

WILF: Have had hunger in my belly all winter, snap of cold on my skin, then a wolf takes my leg, and am beaten and dragged here.

JACOB: Need you to confess Wilf.

WILF: And then?

JACOB: Will heal you up. Feed you. Water you.

WILF: Then dress me in white. Take me to the gallows. And take my head.

Jacob *is silent.*

A confession? Why?

JACOB: You won't suffer. One flick of the sword.

WILF: No suffering there.

JACOB: There's quick suffering, and there's slow.

WILF: Want you to hurt when you do it.

JACOB: Right.

Right.

Jacob *moves away.*

He begins to stretch.

He whirls his shoulders round and round, breathes in and out, makes his body ready.

He faces away from **Wilf**.

You're in this room.

There's a candle.

I'm here.

I've a knife in my hand.

55

The flame flickers in my eye, in your eye.

I can see your eye. White. Black.

You see mine.

You see your face in my eye.

I see mine in yours.

I run the knife over the candle.

I hold it there.

I wait.

Confess.

WILF: No.

JACOB: I take the knife off the flame.

Press it to your skin.

WILF: I won't.

JACOB: You scream.

Red flesh.

Burnt flesh.

Sore.

I put the tip of the knife on your burn.

Put it in just a bit.

Skin has layers.

Knife goes through the first.

A tiny stab.

Confess.

WILF: No.

JACOB: I push.

Through one layer, then another.

Slow, so slow.

Til I'm touching muscle.

Confess.

WILF: Fuck off.

JACOB: I walk away.

WILF: Where?

JACOB: To the corner.

WILF: What's there?

JACOB: Bad things.

I pick one up.

A bad thing.

Candle makes the room hot.

WILF: I can smell my burnt flesh.

JACOB: I can smell your burnt flesh.

I put the bad thing on your finger.

On your nail.

It's heavy.

WILF: Is it?

JACOB: Very. It's a bad thing.

I turn it.

WILF: It pinches.

JACOB: I turn again.

Blood rushes back.

Flesh is white now.

The nail white as well.

A red halo round the thing.

WILF: Stop it.

JACOB: Confess.

I turn again.

WILF: No.

JACOB: Confess.

WILF: Stop.

JACOB: I turn again.

WILF: Jacob.

JACOB: I turn again and again and again.

The nail splits.

WILF: Please.

JACOB: I turn until the skin splits and spits blood.

I turn and turn til I find bone.

Hard.

Yellow.

Small.

But hard.

Crack.

Spit.

Scream.

Through hard bone.

Soft marrow.

The bone beneath the marrow.

Skin opened like a flower.

I press and press and press.

Metal meets metal.

I stop.

Can't turn anymore after that.

Jacob *turns to* **Wilf**.

He waits.

He hears nothing.

He starts to leave.

WILF: Was asleep when they came.

Should've heard.

Something could've been done.

Jacob *breathes in.*

It enough?

Is it enough?

Jacob *nods.*

He leaves.

*

Inside **Hilde** *and* **Jacob's** *house.*

Jacob *stands in the door having just entered.*

He looks at **Hilde**.

She looks at him.

They say nothing.

He spits in his hands, rubs them.

She puts her hand to her mouth.

He finishes cleaning himself.

He goes to a bucket of water and washes his hands again.

He does this slowly.

He dries his hands.

He looks at her.

She comes to and hugs him.

He accepts the hug.

He cries.

She soothes him.

He pushes her off.

He stands still.

She doesn't know what to do.

JACOB: Can you -

Can you still -
After I do it?

Can you?

Cos I've no choice.

Hilde?

HILDE: Chose you Jacob.

JACOB: Look what I've given you.

HILDE: Life!

JACOB: No

Shame.

Death.

HILDE: Hope!

You brought me hope.

Brought them hope.

But there's no healing that town.

Fix this door.

Fix that coop.

Hatch more chickens.

That's enough.

Ana *comes in.*

She sits down.

She is shaking.

Hilde *goes to her.*

She is panicking, breathing hard.

She has blood on her hands.

Ana *continues to panic.*

There's blood on your hands.

Ana *jumps up.*

Sees the blood.

She scrubs her hands frantically on her dress.

ANA: Water.

Ana *scrubs her hands.*

HILDE: Why's there blood on your hands?

ANA: Oh God oh God oh God.

Fuck!

JACOB: Has happened?

HILDE: Ana?

ANA: He was happy.

In his room.

He was happy. Laughing. Back to the same.

Beaten Franz.

Beaten the herdsmen.

So happy.

So I put it in his neck.

A knife.

He held his neck.

Rolled away crying.

Put in again and again and again and again.

All over him.

Cunt bastard.

He looked at me.

I laughed.

Said his cock looked like a woodlouse curling up.

Breath was vinegar and piss.

Hands scaled and sore.

I'm scared.

Hilde *has moved away.*

JACOB: He breathing when you left?

ANA: Eyes open.

Mouth open.

Blood like a lake.

JACOB: He found?

ANA: Not yet. I think.

JACOB: No one saw you?

ANA: It happened deep in the house.

JACOB: Through a window?

ANA: No.

JACOB: Sound?

ANA: Silent.

JACOB: Followed?

ANA: No.

JACOB: Keep your hood up when through the gate?

ANA: Yes and my hands in my cloak.

HILDE: Bring this under our roof?

ANA: Help me.

HILDE: Get out!

JACOB: Wait.

HILDE: Put her in your cell.

ANA: My friends.

HILDE: Friends? You come here with this and call us friends?

JACOB: No one saw her.

HILDE: She's killed! She's killed Hals. Highest man there is. Be coming for her. For us.

JACOB: You must get away.

ANA: Where?

JACOB: Through the woods and out the other side.

ANA: Yes.

Yes.

JACOB: But you must go now.

ANA: Yes.

> Through the woods.
>
> Other cities.
>
> I'll find other cities. On the other side of the trees.
>
> I don't know the way.

HILDE: You keep going until you're out of the woods! Find the sea, your city of white walls or something else. All your big dreams, throw yourself into them. Just get far away from this house!

ANA: Brought here in a cart, slept for days. Never saw the way.

> **Hilde** *forces* **Ana** *to the door.*
>
> **Ana** *gets on her knees.*
>
> Begging you.
>
> Show me the way out.
>
> It's so dark.

JACOB: Go outside. And wait.

> **Ana** *does.*
>
> I can help her.

HILDE: You'll be caught!

JACOB: I won't kill two I've cared for. One is bad enough.

HILDE: Have taken plenty of heads.

JACOB: I have.

> And used to be I could feel clean when I did.
>
> Will not kill for them anymore.

HILDE: What makes you faster and more cunning than them?

JACOB: It is right.

HILDE: Right doesn't make you fast. It makes you foolish!

> We can live here Jacob. We can put those chickens back in a coop.
>
> We can build out the house. You will get coin. We will have a child.

We will live whether hated or not.

There is a dream here that is coming into bloom!

JACOB: If I take her to the cells, then I don't know what it is anymore.

HILDE: This is all for you isn't it? For your soul. Listen to me. A soul doesn't bleed. A soul doesn't give birth. A soul doesn't build a house.

JACOB: A soul loves.

HILDE: Give all that up for her, rash her?

JACOB: Will be back so soon.

Hilde, I promise you -

HILDE: Don't.

JACOB: Will be quick.

HILDE: I won't be here if you're not back this night.

JACOB: Why?

HILDE: I'll know you've been found.

Or that they'll find you.

If you're gone that long.

Nothing'll be here if you take that long, nothing to save. So I'll go and I'll make my own way.

JACOB: Am coming back.

HILDE: Can live without you Jacob. Survive very well on my own. Stay cos I love you. If you're not here, then I won't be. Find my own place in the world. Without you.

JACOB: You know this is right.

HILDE: Don't want to be right Jacob. I want to live wide and happy.

Go.

JACOB: Hilde.

HILDE: Now.

He goes to her, she retreats.

Off with you before I change my mind.

He takes his sword from the wall.

She gets a lantern.

She hands the lantern to **Jacob***.*

He goes to **Hilde***.*

JACOB: All will be well.

Like it says in scripture.

The lion and the wolf and the lamb.

It happened, the world moved.

You read it out loud in this house.

HILDE: I did.

But only you believed it.

They disappear out of sight.

Then.

Dogs.

Lights.

Cries.

*

Inside **Hilde** *and* **Jacob's** *house.*

Franz *has a bandage wrapped around his head.*

FRANZ: Where is she?

HILDE: Not here Franz.

FRANZ: Call me sir!

This outburst catches his tooth, he winces in pain.

HILDE: If it hurts to speak, speak less.

He starts to wretch.

FRANZ: Where's husband?

She gets him a bucket.

He spits and vomits into it.

HILDE: You're not well.

FRANZ: Shut up.

Shut up.

Or I'll have the guard drag you inside the walls.

Dogs followed their scent all the way here. Where've they gone to?

She won't answer.

Know she was helping you. Know you were helping her.

Nice thing about dogs is they don't lie. Wag their tails, happy. Bare their teeth, cross. Point their muzzles, they've smelt and if they've smelt it's as good as seeing.

Sure he's not left you for her?

He gets close, looks her up down.

He steps back.

I'd leave you.

She grabs his face.

He is in so much pain he cannot even cry out.

HILDE: Something to say Franz?

She won't let go.

You'd no idea how strong I was did you? Spent all my life carrying and striving and labouring under the weight of you and that town. All that puts muscle on you. Muscle on my arms, my legs, my fingers. Stronger than you'd ever believe.

She releases him.

He is gasping for air.

She gets him a stool.

She makes him sit down.

She feels his head.

He looks at her.

You're dying.

FRANZ: Bitch.

HILDE: Now now Franz.

FRANZ: Hate this town. Hate the merchants. Hate your husband. Hate you. And I hate sheep. Fucking stink. Always shit, dark brown shit, right round their arse and they stare with black eyes, shit hanging from their arse and then they fall down and can't get up. That's this town, a big sheep stuck in a ditch. Helping up and helping up. Always helping up. No thanks, never! Not from herdsmen, merchants, you, your husband. The dogs piss on my front door. And now a knife's plunged into the biggest man and my executioner runs off with the cunt that did it. Rip it down and sweep it into the river.

He picks up a piece of cloth.

HILDE: That's not yours.

FRANZ: For the dogs, has his smell on him.

HILDE: It's mine.

FRANZ: Is not.

HILDE: Is!

FRANZ: None of this is yours. A house for the executioner. But he's not executioner anymore. He's not even fucking here!

All you see is town's.

He goes round the house.

This is town's.

So's this.

So's this.

All town's.

You're not gone at sun up, you'll be dragged to the stocks, stood in the square and whipped.

She grabs him.

Turns him.

She forces his mouth open.

She rips his tooth out with her bare hands.

He drops to the floor.

She throws his tooth aside.

She stands over him, blood on her hands.

HILDE: See if that heals now.

Likely to die.

Bit less likely now.

Should be grateful.

He lies on the ground gasping through the pain.

Hilde *ignores him.*

She finds a large piece of cloth.

She folds it.

She puts it round her shoulder, under one arm.

It is a bundle.

She quickly puts objects into it...

She picks up her stick.

She puts it under her arm.

She prods **Franz**.

Out of my house.

He gets up.

Out!

He goes out clutching his bleeding mouth.

She turns to **Franz** *and the waiting men and dogs.*

Honoured sirs, this is yours! You are welcome to it!

2.

Pitch black.

Ana *holds the sword and a lantern.*

Jacob *appears.*

She swings the sword.

He avoids it.

She drops the sword.

He takes the lantern from her.

JACOB: D'you run for?

ANA: Am I hurt?

JACOB: Why?

ANA: Have you seen?

JACOB: Seen what?

She's checking herself frantically.

ANA: No no no.

JACOB: Breathe!

ANA: Jacob!

JACOB: Do as I say!

She breathes in.

That's it.

And again.

She does.

Back and forth.

She breathes in and out.

Now.

Has happened?

She checks her body.

ANA: I'm not hurt.

Yes. I'm fine.

JACOB: What you see?

Pig *enters carrying the corpse of a wolf.*

Jacob *gets in front of* **Ana***, points the sword at* **Pig***.*

PIG: Put that down.

JACOB: Who're you?

Howling is heard.

ANA: More of them.

JACOB: Get behind me, you as well.

PIG: Think you can take on a pack?

ANA: Calling for me.

PIG: No, they're in mourning.

Stay put. And don't swing that thing at them.

Pig *disappears.*

JACOB: Wait!

The howling gets louder now.

Jacob *brandishes his sword.*

Stand behind me.

Pig *reappears.*

He has food in his arms.

PIG: Do as Pig says and put your sword on the ground.

The howling is very, very loud now.

Be ripped to pieces if you don't.

Jacob *puts the sword down.*

Pig *puts food on the ground in a circle round them.*

JACOB: Doing?

PIG: Shut up.

He finishes.

Kneel.

Jacob *and* **Ana** *stare at the wolves, who aren't howling anymore, they're silent.*

Do as Pig does!

They kneel.

The wolves approach.

Pig *puts out a hand on the ground, keeping his head bowed.*

A moment.

The wolves eat.

Am so sorry.

The wolves leave.

ANA: How did you do that?

PIG: Do what?

ANA: Command them like a lord.

PIG: Kept it fair. They're in mourning for her, the one you took. So Pig gave them what I had.

He strokes the dead wolf.

Didn't have to do this.

ANA: She snarled at me, lunged at me.

PIG: Was scared.

JACOB: Would you've had her do? Let its jaws on her?

PIG: Not if she'd fed it.

ANA: With what?

PIG: Must have something on you.

ANA: I've nothing.

PIG: Walled-ins're stupider than Pig thought. See her ribs? Your breath weighs more. See, cuts on her face. Needs help. But instead she meets you.

JACOB: It's a wolf.

PIG: We're all wolves out here. All trees. All rabbits. All birds.

Not you though. Not someone high and mighty, walls where your eyes should be. Stamping, ripping, trampling, blind and stupid.

Why?

Why've you come here?

They say nothing.

Pig has given my last food for you. That was all Pig had after a bitter, bitter winter, and spring's not come yet. Fair you say why.

Jacob and **Ana** *look at one another.*

A moment.

ANA: We're walking straight through.

JACOB: To the other side.

PIG: Why?

They don't answer.

Pig *laughs.*

Well, ever you're going, ever the reason, you won't get out.

JACOB: Threat?

PIG: Like you're waving your cock at me, put your sword down, big man.

JACOB: It stays out.

PIG: It's an evil thing.

JACOB: You threaten us, it stays.

PIG: Pig's not threatening, speaking the truth!

JACOB: Which is?

PIG: You won't get out.

JACOB: Why?

PIG: Cos you don't know the law.

JACOB: No law out here.

PIG: Is.

Fair. That's the law out here.

An animal's hungry and you can feed it, you feed it. Do that and you'll get back whatever you've given ten times over. Even if it's your last bite to eat.

Want to live another day out here, you've to know that.

JACOB: Right. Give and give back.

Will remember it.

We're sorry for your loss.

Now we'll be on our way.

And we'll make sure we keep things fair.

PIG: Not the only reason you won't get out.

JACOB: Thought there was one?

PIG: When did Pig say there was one?

JACOB: Well?

PIG: Walk off, a man like you, walled-in, you'll go nowhere but back on yourself, round and round and round.

JACOB: More riddles from the wild man.

PIG: Oh such knowledge the big man has. Well, clever clogs, tell Pig where you are. Go on. Give Pig a sign. You close to town? Or near the other side? Or in the dead middle? Which pack was that? Who's their leader? Know where their den is? Which way will lead you to water, which to the hills?

Thought not.

JACOB: Come on.

Jacob *walks off.*

Ana *hesitates, then follows.*

PIG: Wouldn't go with him, miss.

ANA: I'll go where I please.

PIG: They all come here looking for a way out.

Pig watches them.

Get hungry first. Eat a green berry, spew their guts cos of it. Then they're thirsty. That's when it gets bad. They cry out, beg for water, find none, cry some more, slump in a heap, have their limbs taken by a wolf, or the town and their dogs catch up at last and rip them out of the woods and into the dark belly of the walls.

Pig sees this all the time. Should listen to me.

ANA: And why would we?

PIG: Cos Pig knows how to walk straight. Straight out. Or straight in.

JACOB: You saying?

PIG: You help Pig, Pig'll help you.

A moment.

Ana *steps forward.*

JACOB: Ana -

ANA: D'you want?

PIG: You're wiser than him.

ANA: Speak or I'll go.

PIG: That's fair.

See?

It's a good law isn't it.

ANA: Out with it.

PIG: Right.

Pig needs out.

Used to be wolves followed me round the forest. Ate what I left. Loved me. Would lick my hands clean of the food I gave them.

But this winter, oh it got so cold, Pig had to follow them, not them follow him, Pig had to eat their scraps.

They didn't like that.

So they smelled out my stores.

And when they'd eaten all, one night, not long ago, they ran out the woods, all of them, every pack, one great army, quiet and dark and savage, came back covered in blood and not one of them brought Pig a bite to eat, not a sliver of sheep from outside the walls, half of them dead, the other half with full but skinny bellies and howling all round the woods, not a bite to eat.

Either Pig stays and dies or goes and lives.

But Pig's knowledge falls the second he's out of the trees.

Need someone to show me how to walk down cobbled streets, keep my eyes hooded in walls.

So?

Jacob *and* **Ana** *look at one another.*

ANA: You'll help?

PIG: If you help Pig.

A moment.

JACOB: Show us the way then.

PIG: Want it now?

JACOB: Yes now.

PIG: It's night.

JACOB: We want to move.

PIG: That pack's moving about.

Much safer to stay.

Move when it's light.

Oh and put out the lantern. Don't want us grabbed while we sleep.

*

Next morning.

Light through leaves.

Jacob *wakes.*

JACOB: Where is he?

ANA: Somewhere over there, getting food for the journey.

Said he had some traps set round here. Rabbits he says.

I'd like a bit of rabbit.

JACOB: Should've woken me.

ANA: You needed sleep.

JACOB: Look at the sun, it's late. Far too late.

ANA: It's not.

JACOB: Fuck.

He gets up, paces.

ANA: Jacob?

Jacob, what is it?

JACOB: You trust him?

ANA: Who?

JACOB: Pig.

You trust him to see you out?

ANA: I do.

JACOB: Why?

ANA: Look what he did last night.

He could've left us to be ripped down and picked clean.

But he didn't.

JACOB: Just met the man.

ANA: He gave up his food to save us, I trust him.

JACOB: Know who's in these woods? Bandits, wild men. Outlaws. That's what he is.

ANA: You know nothing of him.

He knows these woods Jacob.

We don't.

JACOB: You might not, I do. And I know how to swing a sword, set a bone. Know how that town works. Not you. You don't know a thing, just stabbing and ripping, do it as you see fit.

ANA: Saying?

JACOB: You brought me here Ana. Your knife in his neck pushed me into the trees.

Should have thought of Hilde and me before you killed Hals.

ANA: I had to.

JACOB: It was working.

ANA: It was not.

JACOB: It was a start.

ANA: It wasn't enough.

JACOB: You wouldn't let it run.

ANA: Cos I'm not scared.

JACOB: And I'm not rash.

ANA: You're a coward!

JACOB: And you're a fool!

A while.

I'm gone one night and she'll be gone.

That's what she said.

And it's morning now.

ANA: She said this?

JACOB: It matter to you if she did or not?

ANA: It shames me.

If she said this, you must leave.

Go to her.

JACOB: Ordering me to leave?

ANA: Am not ordering, am begging.

JACOB: Have left everything to get you safe, can't just go and leave you with him.

ANA: It is my choice to make.

JACOB: You swung at that wolf. You stabbed your husband. You stole grain. Have made many choices Ana. And it's mine to see you out.

ANA: It is Pig's. You're not needed.

JACOB: You'd be in the cells if not for me.

ANA: And if she's in the cells?

JACOB: Then we'd have put her there.

A moment.

I have to go.

ANA: Jacob.

I'm not sorry for Hals.

But -

I will get out, Pig will do what I say, I promise you this.

JACOB: But I'm lost too Ana.

ANA: I'll have him tell you the way.

Pig *enters with a wolf-skin.*

He offers the skin to **Ana**.

She doesn't take it.

PIG: Suit yourself.

He drapes the skin over himself.

ANA: Nearly in tears over her last night.

PIG: Sadder would be to let her go to waste. She keeps us warm, we honour her.

Now who's after you?

They don't answer.

Think it's fair Pig knows.

ANA: You're getting a new life, with me to guide you, don't need to know a thing.

PIG: Pig's a lucky pup, yes. A highborn like you to guide him.

But that's what puzzles him.

What're you doing out here with the executioner?

Nothing.

Don't try silence. Never covers anything.

JACOB: How?

PIG: Who else has a square-edged blade? It's for taking heads, Mr Executioner.

Question is what you've done.

She your prisoner?

Are you in love?

That's a good story. Kind of story brother'd tell round a fire to keep the fear of the dark away.

The executioner and the woman he loved.

A moment.

ANA: I'm wanted. He helped me escape.

JACOB: And I'm to my wife.

Who I love.

PIG: Love her so much you left her?

JACOB: Shut up.

PIG: Fair enough.

So you're leaving, she's with me.

Want me to point you the way back?

JACOB: How do I know you'll help her?

ANA: Jacob -

JACOB: Need to know.

Well?

PIG: You can trust Pig.

JACOB: Saying's easy.

PIG: Pig likes things fair.

JACOB: More words.

PIG: You're to home, why d'you care?

JACOB: Not leaving unless I know you'll be true.

PIG: What you do?

ANA: I killed my husband.

PIG: Why?

ANA: He was a big man, powerful man and he was evil.

PIG: Can't kill just cos something's nasty. Otherwise slugs and spiders'd be gone from the face of the earth.

ANA: He was a merchant. Biggest one in the walls.

One of those fat bastards that bring carts through the woods.

Think they're strong cos they've a big sack of coin and men who'll beat and kill to protect them.

He starved his people who lived outside and guarded his property and gave them nothing in return.

I took him down.

PIG: Very fair.

And you saved her. Why?

JACOB: She's a friend.

PIG: Just that, Mr Executioner?

JACOB: I'm not executioner anymore.

I couldn't be.

So I ran.

Town has no one to keep the peace.

And I wasn't killing. I was healing.

The more I healed, the more it hurt the merchants.

Pig *takes this in.*

PIG: Pig hates town.

Those who steal cos they're hungry. Those who need help but get none. Woods are where they usually end up.

Thing is, they're mostly running from you, Mr Executioner.

JACOB: I'm not that anymore.

PIG: But you were.

They come here and then they're found and brought back and have their heads taken or a noose wrapped tight round their necks until SNAP!

Wasn't always like that.

People'd come to us and we'd let them come. People who needed to leave. People who town wanted. People who wanted more from the world. Town'd let them be. They weren't going back. Were never any harm to that town.

We'd chop down trees, grow crops, build houses, love, grow old, die, bury our dead.

Was good.

Then town changed its mind, new Justice wanted the woods cleared up, all those naughty people living in the trees taken care of.

So they took the men, the women, left the children. Said we were outlaws, wolves. Can do whatever you like to a wolf. Hunt it, skin it, cage it.

Cut off its head.

Must've been your father did that to us.

A moment.

JACOB: Remember.

Father didn't speak for weeks.

ANA: Jacob made it fair.

He helped me rip down those walls.

He's not walking back to the same town today.

That's cos of him.

Will you help me honestly?

Pig *nods.*

Ana *goes to* **Jacob**.

ANA: Been thinking, if they find you, and if they've found her, you can tell them you were hunting me, but you lost me or something.

JACOB: I'll think of something.

ANA: You talked them into making you healer.

Was you did that.

They embrace.

JACOB: Which way Pig?

PIG: See that tree with red moss on it in the distance?

JACOB: Yes.

PIG: Follow that line and you'll be back in half a day.

JACOB: Right.

PIG: Hurry, town's after you, so there're dogs're on the trail.

JACOB: Goodbye.

ANA: Bye.

Jacob *goes.*

Pig *gives her a moment.*

So.

Where're those rabbits?

PIG: You know what to do with them?

ANA: Roast them on a fire?

Pig *laughs, shakes his head.*

ANA: What then?

PIG: Gut them, skin them, clean them, then stick them on a fire.

Know how to do that?

ANA: Course not.

PIG: How high up were you?

ANA: Not from town, came from the sea.

PIG: Climb out of it like some terrible mermaid?

ANA: A port. Boats from all over coming in and out.

PIG: Go there once we're out?

ANA: Go anywhere you like. World's very big.

PIG: Frightening.

ANA: I'll show you.

PIG: Good. Cos Pig doesn't know how to use a fork. Think we meet each other in the middle.

ANA: Should move.

There's a cry of pain.

JACOB: Help!

Ana *runs off.*

Ana *drags* **Jacob** *on.*

ANA: Help me!

Pig *rolls his eyes, goes to help.*

Jacob's *leg is badly hurt, lots of blood.*

PIG: Happened?

JACOB: A snare.

ANA: One of yours?

Pig *looks.*

PIG: Only put two down. Could be an old one from a hunter. Would never leave a snare to trap and kill an animal without eating it.

JACOB: Take my shoe off.

Slow!

She does.

Move the toe.

She does.

The ankle.

She does.

He flexes his toes.

It's not broken.

ANA: Swollen.

JACOB: Be fine.

ANA: There's a deep cut.

JACOB: Can walk.

He stands.

ANA: Don't!

He walks off a way, trips, cries out.

Ana *goes to him.*

He pushes her away.

JACOB: Let me.

ANA: Jacob!

He tries to take a step.

He can't put any weight on it.

He sits down.

JACOB: I can't walk.

ANA: You will. We'll get you back to her.

JACOB: If I sit it'll get better. You should go.

ANA: No.

JACOB: Will get better if I sit for a bit.

ANA: It won't.

PIG: Got men after you, we should leave.

ANA: No.

JACOB: He's right.

ANA: Won't show you the world otherwise.

PIG: They'll find you, find us.

ANA: Must be a way.

Come on Pig.

JACOB: Don't.

ANA: It's what's fair.

Pig *snarls.*

JACOB: Leave me here. You can't carry me.

PIG: Pig can.

We'll have to move every sun up.

And he needs yarrow.

JACOB: Yarrow?

PIG: Keep the wound clean. That's what'll get you. Rot. Nothing else.

JACOB: It's not broken, needs nothing but water.

PIG: Don't know about bones, but know about cuts going green.

JACOB: Where's this yarrow?

PIG: Not come through yet. Will be soon. Can feel spring turning. Need your ankle clean for the next week.

Now we must move.

ANA: I'll cover our tracks with a branch or something.

PIG: Taught you that?

ANA: Thought of it just now.

PIG: Make a wild woman out of you yet.

Right!

Hold on tight, Mr Executioner.

JACOB: No.

ANA: Jacob be quiet.

JACOB: Won't let you.

ANA: Pick him up Pig.

Pig *slings* **Jacob** *over his back.*

PIG: Christ.

JACOB: Ana!

ANA: You're coming with us. Am sending you back to Hilde alive and well.

Pig *walks off.*

Ana *follows.*

*

A cell.

HILDE: That guard feeding you?

WILF: Yes.

HILDE: Don't lie. Could play your ribs like a harp.

He hurt you? Show me.

WILF: I look that bad?

HILDE: No -

WILF: Cos you look well.

HILDE: Don't lie!

WILF: Not lying.

HILDE: Don't feel it.

Feel.

Angry.

Like to rip that guard's head off and kick a hole in the door, carry you out and throw you over the wall.

WILF: No one's that strong. Except giants.

HILDE: Like to be a giant.

WILF: Me too.

HILDE: Stomp the walls down, squash the merchants.

WILF: Kick them.

HILDE: Yes! Hard as a horse. They'd shoot through the air like canon balls.

A moment.

Saw them taking you.

Should've got my knife. Stabbed and slashed and fought. They'd never have got you in here.

WILF: Why you here?

HILDE: Had to.

She shudders.

Haven't been inside these walls since I walked out of them a married woman.

People stared.

Executioner's wife.

Parents never came to our wedding.

Guard to the keep let me in though. Nice man. Gave him a few eggs. A figure I'd carved. It's of a dog, for his child, if he has one.

And, well, he let me in.

A moment.

Jacob'd come home from this place every day.

Never once got jealous that he walked these streets. Hated living here.

He'd come home, wash his hands, not say a word and I'd never ask him what happened in here.

We kept this room in dark and silence.

I put you here.

WILF: Hals put me here, Franz put me here.

HILDE: I would've let him kill you -

WILF: Hilde -

HILDE: I was going to stay in that house and live on after you -

WILF: Stop -

HILDE: You have to hear -

WILF: Don't.

HILDE: Let me.

WILF: You're Hilde.

Friend.

Want it to stay like that.

HILDE: But -

WILF: All I have.

A moment.

HILDE: Have they given you a day?

WILF: Yes.

HILDE: When?

A moment.

WILF: Know he's gone.

A moment.

HILDE: How?

WILF: He never came back.

And now you're here.

Is he?

A moment.

HILDE: Ana killed Hals.

WILF: Why?

HILDE: Cos you were taken.

WILF: Happened?

HILDE: She came to our house for help. Took her to the woods, to safety. Supposed to come back but before he could climb back through our door and put the light out and fall into bed, town came with dogs. So much quicker than we thought.

WILF: What of town?

HILDE: Holding its breath.

Franz took my house from me.

So I ripped his tooth out.

With my bare hands.

He's up there. Very sick. So much green pus came out of his mouth. Dying.

There are guards at the gates and by the tents. Looking at the herdsmen.

Herdsmen're looking back at the guards.

Merchants're pacing the walls, looking down at all of them.

All of them waiting for Franz to die, a new Justice to be chosen and Jacob and Ana to be brought back and killed.

Wilf *takes this in.*

WILF: Didn't turn her in?

HILDE: He wanted her to live.

WILF: But.

She killed. Can do anything if you've enough height.

HILDE: He couldn't do it anymore.

WILF: But fine to put me in this cell, skin me, take my head!

Didn't even have the kindness to cut my throat.

HILDE: Stop.

WILF: He could've given me that one thing.

Spared me before making off with her! Fuck didn't you make him do it?!

HILDE: Wilf?

WILF: Why why why why whhhhyyyyyyyy?!

She comforts him.

HILDE: Wilf?

You can tell me Wilf.

Whatever it is.

WILF: Can't.

A while.

Been asked to take his place.

She looks at him.

Told me what he'd do to me. So I confessed.

Felt it end.

But he never came back. No one did. Not a for a few days.

Guard brought food, water, but never said a word.

Til one day guard spoke.

Merchants need an executioner.

Gave me time to think on it.

But if a herdsman steals or kills or riots, then I must choose quick, else they'll ask some other poor man and he'll take my head instead

Should've begged him to stay.

It matter? I'm dead both ways. Executed or executioner.

HILDE: You decided?

WILF: No one's rioted yet, so it hangs over me.

Herdsmen gets dragged in, no idea what I'll do.

Are they calm?

HILDE: Yes.

WILF: Said there were guards watching them.

HILDE: Still hungry. Healing gone.

WILF: They'll attack then. Or try to leap the walls. Be holding one of their heads soon.

There's a rope in front of me, hands are itching to grab but don't want to, but I'm reaching out anyway. I'll touch it but have no idea if it'll wrap round my neck or pull me up to new life, so alive, so, so well, but in this room, not as prisoner, as Jacob, but not him, me, me in this room with a knife and a flame and a rope and doing things to neighbours, friends, such awful things and then with a sword taking their heads in one clean stroke.

See it all. Right here in this room.

He stood right there. Told me what he does. Right where you're standing.

Saw my eyes in his. See them when I sleep. Him and me. And I look like him. And he looks like me.

A while.

HILDE: Still have the chickens. And a bundle. Everything I need.

Built a little shelter.

WILF: Course you did.

HILDE: Been making little shoes out of twigs. Like a basket for your feet. Stops me sinking through the mud. Can walk anywhere with them.

HILDE: You going to say yes?

WILF: Die if I don't.

A while.

HILDE: Do nothing.

WILF: Nothing?

HILDE: Until you have to.

Jacob and me and Ana thinking what's to happen next is what got you in this cell.

Far too much of that.

You're to wait.

And I will not let a single herdsman come in those cells.

WILF: How?

HILDE: Am going to heal them.

And what're you to do?

WILF: Hilde -

HILDE: Say it.

WILF: Nothing.

HILDE: I will keep them calm.

WILF: Gives me a few days.

HILDE: A few days is everything.

She makes to go.

WILF: Hilde.

HILDE: Will come back soon.

WILF: Promise?

HILDE: Yes.

And you are to do?

WILF: Nothing.

She rips a bit of cloth from her clothes.

HILDE: Take this.

He does.

What'll you do with this?

WILF: Put it on the floor.

HILDE: Stand on it.

WILF: Skate.

HILDE: You're going to skate down a river. Imagine the crowds and the sun on the ice. Skating and flying away.

You're going to do nothing but skate.

A few weeks later.

The woods.

Jacob *is wrapped in the in the wolfskin, asleep.*

Ana *is making a snare.*

Pig *enters.*

She doesn't see him

He watches her work.

He comes closer.

ANA: Lord!

PIG: Sorry.

ANA: How many times must I tell to say if you're near?

PIG: Last time. Promise.

ANA: Heard a dog barking.

PIG: They're not near.

ANA: Still on our tail?

PIG: Oh yes.

But you're lucky.

ANA: Oh yes?

PIG: You've got Pig and Pig's the best at hiding in the whole wood.

ANA: How close?

PIG: Day away.

A moment.

Good snare.

ANA: Saw a rabbit hole nearby.

PIG: Pig likes rabbit.

How's Mr Executioner?

ANA: Stop calling him that.

PIG: It's what he is.

ANA: He's our friend.

PIG: Your friend.

ANA: Then he's yours as well.

　　You carry him every day.

PIG: Pig's back hurts.

ANA: Yet you carry him faithfully.

PIG: You're going to help Pig, so Pig helps you.

ANA: Well it's good of you.

PIG: His leg still pink and clean?

　　She doesn't answer.

　　That's not a good silence.

ANA: A fever today.

　　His wound's going bad.

PIG: Well...

　　It won't be bad anymore.

ANA: So sure of that?

　　Pig *produces some flowers.*

PIG: These'll stop all that. Soon Pig'll have a unladen back, skipping through these trees and all the way out the other side.

　　Ana *examines the flowers*

ANA: Is this - ?

PIG: Yes, yarrow.

　　Like Pig promised.

ANA: Thank God.

PIG: Thank the Sun, not God.

Just started to pop up, little bits of summer.

ANA: This'd better work, Pig.

He shows her his arm.

PIG: See this.

Wolf got Pig there. Pig's fault, got too close.

Yarrow kept it pink and healed.

Be leaving soon, works as quick as the wind.

ANA: You learn all this?

PIG: You know how to walk streets, Pig knows how to walk trees.

ANA: But to know its effect?

PIG: Dad taught me. His dad taught him. His him. On and on backwards.

Pig's brother was specially good with herbs.

ANA: Where is he?

PIG: Town took him away two winters ago.

Mr Executioner over there did for him.

He named me, my brother.

Said I was pink and loud when born, so Pig. Pig of the woods. Last to live here. Last to say goodbye.

Will I like it out there?

ANA: It's a big world, Pig.

PIG: Don't want to get walled in.

ANA: If we're stuck in one place, we'll hunt out another.

PIG: Like the sound of that.

ANA: Go anywhere. Towns. Rivers. The sea.

PIG: Cross the water?

ANA: If you like.

PIG: You'll show me how?

ANA: D'you want me to?

PIG: Oh yes.

ANA: We'll dive into towns and fields. I'll teach you town, you teach me
   outside.

PIG: 'll we do?

ANA: Hunt. Forage.

PIG: Not buy and sell?

ANA: Can do that with what we get.

   And we can steal.

PIG: Yes!

ANA: Run before we're caught. Live as we please. Wild and free. All the
   world a wood!

   Jacob *wakes.*

JACOB: Ana.

   She goes to him.

ANA: You sleep well?

JACOB: Saw Hilde on a rack, her arms behind her, breaking.

ANA: She's alive.

JACOB: Does it smell?

ANA: No.

JACOB: It will soon.

   He tries to stand.

ANA: Stop!

JACOB: Can walk. Know I can.

PIG: You can't.

   Jacob *slumps back.*

   Told you.

ANA: God you're an awful patient.

JACOB: Patient? What healing's going on?

ANA: He's found yarrow.

JACOB: Yarrow? How'll that work?

ANA: He's used it before.

JACOB: I've never used it.

ANA: You not going to try it?

JACOB: No.

ANA: Then you're done for.

Never heal up.

Never get back to her.

You want that?

A silence.

Give it him Pig.

PIG: Have to grind it up and put it in water.

JACOB: Tea? You're giving me tea?

PIG: It's good tea.

Pig *produces a leather bottle.*

He takes a stone.

He puts the flowers on it.

He grinds them, making a paste.

He puts the paste in the bottle.

He offers **Jacob** *the yarrow tea.*

Will help.

JACOB: D'you know about healing?

PIG: More than you.

JACOB: You don't.

ANA: Drink it, Jacob.

Jacob *drinks.*

JACOB: Leg hurts.

ANA: You anything for that?

PIG: Oh yes.

JACOB: Unless you've a barrel of beer, there's nothing for it.

PIG: Not true.

JACOB: What then?

PIG: Pig doesn't have it here.

   But knows where to find it.

JACOB: Course you do.

PIG: Not want it?

ANA: Find it.

   Pig *leaves.*

ANA: Oh Jacob.

JACOB: I feel better.

   A bit.

ANA: We'll get you better.

   We will.

JACOB: But if I don't.

   If I stay like this.

   Promise you'll leave.

ANA: Pig'll fix you.

   She touches his forehead.

   You're starting to cool.

JACOB: Am I?

ANA: Soon you'll be on your feet.

   I promise.

   Think of her.

Think of your life together.

A big wide world where you'll be happy and do whatever you want.

JACOB: She was so brave. First time I saw her in Franz's house I knew she was brave.

Told her that as soon as we were wed she'd be looked at like me. Apart. We left church, side chapel, went through the gates and she took my hand and never once looked back at town.

Looked at me instead.

Want her to see me, want to see her.

He tries to stand.

She puts a hand out, he waves it away.

He stands, he takes a step.

ANA: How is it?

JACOB: Agony, but I think I'll be walking on it soon.

Pig *enters with a piece of bark.*

PIG: You're up!

Pig's got what you need.

Gnaw on that.

ANA: See?

*

The cell.

WILF: You've been too long!

HILDE: Lower your voice.

WILF: Why?

HILDE: We're leaving.

WILF: How?

HILDE: It's like an angel put it in my head. Nearly passed out laughing when it came to me.

When I left my house I took Jacob's coat.

And inside it was a key. For this place. For all of it!

Of course there was. He worked here every day.

How did I think not to look?

So I did. It was there. And here I am.

Come on.

WILF: No.

HILDE: Stop being thick.

WILF: They'll see.

HILDE: It's dark.

WILF: The guard.

HILDE: Not here.

WILF: Guards at the gate.

HILDE: Don't know you.

WILF: Was dragged here by them.

HILDE: They don't recognise me. Me! Executioner's wife.

WILF: Hilde -

HILDE: It's true.

When walked here last not a single one glanced my way.

WILF: Came to find me.

HILDE: Cos they knew where you were, not who you were. Not by sight.

No one inside these walls recognises a soul from outside. Least of all the guards, the merchants. Herdsmen're one big pack to them, same as they couldn't tell one sheep from another.

Only insider who ever recognised me was Franz. And that's cos I cleaned his floors.

Know where Franz is? In the ground. Dead.

WILF: Find this empty they'll look for me.

HILDE: Be gone by then.

WILF: Where?

HILDE: Over the hill and far away!

Herdsmen'll keep it secret.

WILF: Not if they're tortured.

HILDE: Will, cos these last weeks I have healed and healed and healed. And given them eggs. And will give them my chickens and Dick the cockerel too, so they can breed more and get their own eggs!

Now come on.

He stays still.

Want me to put a ring through your nose and drag you out?

WILF: Don't want to.

A moment.

HILDE: Franz is dead. D'you hear me?

The merchants're choosing a new Justice tomorrow.

They'll make you executioner within the day.

The door's open but soon it'll shut.

WILF: Going to refuse. When they ask.

HILDE: And lose your head.

WILF: Yes.

HILDE: Want to stay?

WILF: It's my home.

HILDE: It's dead.

WILF: Then make it new.

HILDE: Not this town.

Have to make and move and find your own little world.

You come with me and we'll find it together.

WILF: Want it here or else nowhere.

HILDE: Why?

WILF: They take my head, that shows who these merchants are.

I leave? That says there's no hope.

HILDE: You're as worthy as Jacob.

WILF: Am nothing like him.

HILDE: Doing a good mime!

You've got to take what's yours and live as well as you can. That's what I do. Already built a bigger shelter for myself. And I will build a bigger one far away.

WILF: Stay. Build one here. Or tear the walls down.

Or leave.

Go where you must. I stay.

HILDE: Have worked day and night to keep the herdsmen calm. Worked small miracles on them. Healed a woman who coughed up her lungs. Stopped a baby dying.

A moment.

I don't know anyone else, Wilf.

Can't go alone.

Can't do it alone.

WILF: Let's stay and build something.

You can heal them.

You fixed my leg, not Jacob.

You're better than him. You are.

And we can make things better.

HILDE: How?

WILF: You heal. I get my lot together. Those inside the walls'll have to listen.

Or leave forever and I'll hang.

HILDE: You've put me in a vice.

WILF: Good'll come.

HILDE: Better.

*

The woods.

Ana *is making a snare.*

She can't quite figure it out.

PIG: Nearly there.

ANA: Going to help me?

PIG: Pig's shown you how.

She gets the knot right this time.

Good.

Now you can get us more rabbits.

ANA: Tired of rabbit.

PIG: You want then?

ANA: Pheasant, woodcock, grouse.

PIG: Fine things.

ANA: You'll eat them too. And cheese.

PIG: Cheese?

ANA: Never heard of cheese?

PIG: Sounds like a sickness.

ANA: Much to learn Pig.

PIG: Is it?

ANA: Milk gone old and hard.

PIG: Not rotten?

ANA: Well, no.

PIG: Must be if it's old.

ANA: It is rotten, but it's also not.

PIG: Sounds horrid.

ANA: You'll like it.

PIG: Won't.

ANA: Well, you'll have time to try it soon. How many days?

PIG: Ten.

If we're quick.

ANA: And how long for Jacob to get back to town?

PIG: He's been gone a day, so... one more, even with him hobbling on a stick.

We'll be eating cheese soon.

ANA: And having a bath. In an inn.

PIG: Is that?

ANA: Oh Pig, you'd be better off teaching me the name of every plant.

Pig *stands.*

Is it?

He motions for her to be quiet.

Get your knife.

She draws it.

She sees someone.

ANA: Jacob?

She puts her knife away.

Jacob *enters with his sword on his back.*

Happened?

Jacob *rushes to* **Pig***, grabs his arm, twists, puts him in a half nelson.*

JACOB: Did you do?

ANA: Let him go.

> **Ana** *grabs* **Jacob,** *pulls him off.*
>
> **Pig** *steps back.*
>
> **Jacob** *hits him.*
>
> **Ana** *draws her knife, holds it to* **Jacob's** *throat.*
>
> Calm yourself.
>
> **Jacob** *puts his sword down.*
>
> Better.
>
> Now.
>
> Has happened?

JACOB: You've got town on your tail.

> Got half a day from here and found a camp. Town guard. Dogs.
>
> Were talking about him. Yes, about you Pig.
>
> Dogs were roaming.
>
> Smelled me.
>
> Had to kill one. The noise. They followed.

PIG: God.

ANA: What's he saying, Pig?

> Pig what's he saying?

PIG: Where are they?

JACOB: Half a day that way, where you pointed me.

PIG: You need to run Ana.

ANA: Has happened?

PIG: Weren't supposed to be so close. Said it so clear!

ANA: What have you done?

PIG: Just run please run.

ANA: Tell me.

PIG: Pig can't.

She grabs him, puts her knife to his throat.

ANA: Speak.

PIG: No.

A moment.

ANA: How do I do it?

A moment.

JACOB: Put it on his forehead, the blade, full length of it.

She does.

Ask him.

ANA: You do?

PIG: Run!

JACOB: Push the blade in.

She does.

Ask him again.

ANA: You do?

Pig *is sobbing.*

Jacob?

JACOB: Now the point. Put it to one side above the eye then push it soft through the skin til you meet the skull.

She does.

Ask him again.

ANA: What did you do?

Pig *stays quiet.*

JACOB: Next you'll slice across then pull the skin back.

But first, ask him again.

ANA: Well Pig?

Nothing.

JACOB: Do it.

Ana *starts to slice.*

Pig *screams.*

PIG: I'll talk I'll talk.

Ana *stops.*

Pig was saving you from them.

ANA: Saving me from who?

PIG: From town!

She lets **Pig** *go.*

PIG: Was so good here before his town came. You'd've loved it. Always laughter in these trees back then.

Then his lot comes.

Took everyone but Pig and his brother. We got to stay.

Got to stay if we told them when outlaws came into the woods.

How d'you think they'd get runaways from the woods, Mr Executioner. Was Pig. Showing town the way or talking to a merchant if they came through, or their workers when they took a cart through the woods.

Pig and his brother wanted to stay. Would've done anything to stay.

JACOB: Why you saving her then?

PIG: Brother and Pig were hungry once. Brother had a thought. And Pig said yes to it. Should never've said yes to it.

He slipped out the trees, took a sheep and brought it here.

Town followed.

Pig and his brother hid. They found my brother. Pig stayed hidden.

Off he went.

To you.

You took my brother's head.

So Pig crept out and told them I'd got their executioner.

Kept you in place by setting a snare for your leg. Ripped your leg right up.

Then I took you up and down and round, just near the edge of the woods.

Last night, slipped away, was so easy, told them where to find you. But not today. Tomorrow.

ANA: You're their pet.

PIG: The coin we fetched for him! Think what use you'd have put that to on the other side of these woods.

ANA: How much?

PIG: Here.

He shows her a small purse of coins.

She laughs.

ANA: Silver.

PIG: Coin.

ANA: Should be gold if it's to go any distance you stupid, stupid man.

PIG: Sorry.

ANA: You are the stupidest of all the stupid men I've met. From my father, to my husband, to you. All cowards using me to make their dreams come true.

Should have your head on a spike.

Distant cries of dogs on the scent.

Here they are.

Take him, Jacob.

JACOB: No.

ANA: Why come back if not to take his head?

JACOB: For all he's done, he's your best chance of getting out.

ANA: Should die for this.

JACOB: Not killing anymore.

ANA: I will.

JACOB: Fine.

He gives her his sword.

Never goes away.

ANA: Have killed.

JACOB: Not like this.

She goes to **Pig**, **Pig** *kneels, she raises the sword, she can't bring herself to swing.*

She puts the sword down.

Jacob *sits down.*

ANA: Get up!

JACOB: They want me.

ANA: It's me they want.

JACOB: Want someone.

Let it be me.

ANA: Oh, lying down on your sword, nailed to a cross, burning on a fire! Act like a beast and run!

Could fight them. You're strong.

Let's die with our teeth in their legs!

JACOB: Haven't fixed a thing if you don't leave.

The dogs are loud now.

She hesitates.

She gives **Jacob** *his sword.*

She goes to **Pig**.

ANA: Show me out.

Pig *grabs her legs.*

PIG: Sorry.

ANA: Get up.

Take me out the woods, I'll show you to the next town, then we're done.

She turns to **Jacob**.

Goodbye.

Ana *and* **Pig** *leave.*

Hilde *and* **Wilf** *enter, they carry a bucket, cloth.*

They approach a man, lying sick on the ground.

Hilde *touches his forehead.*

She thinks, makes a diagnosis.

JACOB: Hilde.

WILF: He's in a trance.

HILDE: It's his fever.

Pass water, a cloth.

Wilf *does.*

She soothes the sick man's brow.

Give me the bag.

JACOB: Love you.

HILDE: Yes yes.

Wilf *has passed a small pouch.*

She takes herbs from it.

She puts them on the man's lips.

She helps him to drink.

This should calm him at least.

WILF: Spoke to the head man today.

HILDE: What he say?

WILF: They're getting a group together. Just like I told him. Old men and women.

They're going to the gates and ask for land.

HILDE: If town says no.

WILF: Here's what I told them: if they don't grant it, then we're sitting down until we get it.

HILDE: The old ones?

WILF: All of us.

HILDE: Until when?

WILF: Til they give us what we need.

My idea that.

HILDE: How'll that work?

WILF: Nothing gets done, they'll see they need us happy if they're to get any coin.

JACOB: Miss you.

HILDE: This one's not well.

Should get sticks and build up the fire, sweat it out of him.

WILF: Once we've got land, can build a place for the sick.

HILDE: Yes.

Have a house again.

WILF: All have houses.

HILDE: Yes.

There is a noise outside.

Cries of triumph...

...barking dogs...

Is that?

Go see.

Wilf *goes.*

Hilde *strokes the sick man.*

JACOB: My darling.

HILDE: Hush now.

WILF: A man in a cart.

Hilde *goes to look.*

HILDE: It's him.

3.

A cell.

Jacob *is blindfolded and tied to a chair.*

A while...

Hilde *enters.*

She carries a bucket of water, a candle, cloth.

She sets her things down, walks towards him, takes off his blindfold.

A while.

JACOB: Time is it?

HILDE: You want to know the time? Not how I am? No hello?

JACOB: So good to see you.

A moment.

HILDE: 's night.

JACOB: Know it's night -

HILDE: Why ask if you know?

JACOB: How long til the sun?

HILDE: Moon's up high.

JACOB: Is it out all of itself or do clouds cover its face?

HILDE: Should I tell you?

JACOB: Costs nothing to tell the moon.

HILDE: Maybe if you give me something. But you've nothing to give. Or've you a pile of gold up your arse?

JACOB: Been here fourteen nights.

HILDE: Know everything don't you?

JACOB: Glass of beer at night as when I ran these cells. Last I drank was beer. It's night.

HILDE: Why ask if you know it all?

JACOB: Between each meal's a season to me. Much time've I got?

What can I give for you to tell me?

HILDE: Filthy. Stink. Shit and blood down your legs. Nothing you can give and nothing I'd take from your hands if you could.

JACOB: Is something.

's a small thing.

Want you to have it.

Sorry.

HILDE: Shut your face, don't want your sorry! Keep it it tucked in your guts to rot and die. A sorry for the moon!

JACOB: Give it free.

HILDE: You left. Told you not but you still left. No way it would lead to anything but trouble. Always the fucking hero!

No sorry's enough for all that.

A moment.

JACOB: Didn't think you'd come.

HILDE: Didn't want to.

JACOB: But you did.

HILDE: They asked for me. Found me. Told me to come. Said I'd be banished if I didn't.

JACOB: Hilde, Hilde I never -

HILDE: Shut. Up.

A while.

JACOB: They give you a knife?

She laughs.

HILDE: Torture you? Looks like they've done enough of that. Me torture you? No.

Don't want to touch you. Think if I touch you I'll be sick.

But they want me to touch you.

114

Not torture you.

Just.

Wash you. Want me to wash you. Wouldn't have a single man or woman touch the filth of you. Not even the gaoler, the cook, the prisoner next door, the gravedigger, a foreign wretch with no teeth, a whore on the street. Not even the man who'll take your head when the sun's up.

Just me.

Wash that blood off your face. Clean the cuts on your back. Put a sweet smell over your sores. Get you looking half way to heavenly before your head's held up for all to see.

And if I don't. If you're not clean when I leave. If you're not on my hands, your blood and pus on my hands. Out I go, the road and the woods for me.

Could though. Torture you.

She goes to him, grabs his hair.

Could pull til the roots come out and blood trickles over your eyes. Or put my finger deep in the cut, wriggle it like a worm on a hook til you're full of screams and spit and your eyes roll in the sockets. Stick my finger deep into you and pull at the skin and muscle. Wrap my hands round your bones and tug til they snaps inside and the sharp ends poke out the skin. They never said I couldn't.

I'd clean you after. Such care. Cloths to mop the blood. Set the bones, slip them back into place with a crack. Get the muck off your back, legs, arms, head. Put fine oil through your hair. A new shirt on your back. And tomorrow when the sun rises watch them take your head and see your blood kick all over that nice clean cloth.

Could do that.

She pulls him up by his hair just enough.

He winces.

She lets him go.

He sinks down.

You stink.

She goes to the bucket, picks up the cloth, brings it to him.

She sets the bucket down.

She throws the cloth on the floor, she can't bring herself to do it.

She laughs to herself.

Why'm I?

Can't.

Won't.

JACOB: You must.

HILDE: Piss on their orders.

JACOB: Wash me and you'll be safe.

You're free of me tomorrow Hilde.

HILDE: Never wanted to be free of you. Cannot stand the thought of being free of you. But you left to be a good man.

JACOB: They came so quick.

Was to be a short hop to the woods and back. No one would ever know.

HILDE: Their dogs tracked you to our door.

No matter if they'd come quickly or not, you'd've been strung up and me next to you.

JACOB: She came to our door.

HILDE: Most others would have taken her life if it meant a chance at happiness. But you had to save her.

JACOB: It was right.

HILDE: Right for her to kill?

JACOB: Town is better now it's rid of Hals.

Did they catch her?

A moment.

HILDE: No.

One thing you did that went well.

JACOB: I wanted to come back.

HILDE: To what? They took the house.

JACOB: It's yours.

HILDE: No, it's the executioner's house. And you're not the executioner anymore.

JACOB: Where've you stayed?

Are you hungry?

You've a roof?

HILDE: Yes.

And a fire for my pot.

Chickens that sleep nuzzled up to me.

Eggs they lay I sell.

And the best thing I've ever made. A sling. One piece of cloth, so simple, tied on the shoulder, carry my whole life in that, bend like a tree branch in a storm and always remain standing.

Carry whatever I please, whatever my mind brings to me.

I'm healer as well.

Outside these walls I am healer. You left and I missed you and I raged and I cried and then I found something, something that lasts, I made something.

Wilf's alive. He's in the tents. The merchants don't care where he is.

He has big dreams.

They've given the herdsmen land. Crops'll be planted in a week or so, when spring gets into step.

I'm helping.

JACOB: Town's fixed.

Town is fixed.

HILDE: Not for me it isn't.

You're back. I could lose it all.

JACOB: Forget me. Be gone tomorrow.

A new town, Hilde.

HILDE: Stop being the martyr, Jacob!

JACOB: Scripture says all will be well.

HILDE: Only if we make it so.

Cannot wait for it.

Waiting's what kills.

JACOB: But you're healer.

HILDE: If I wash you.

JACOB: Then you must.

HILDE: Don't heal for them inside!

Heal for those outside.

Not cos they asked, but cos I chose.

JACOB: Then swallow this one thing.

HILDE: SHUT UP.

This settles.

JACOB: Who'll take my head?

HILDE: Picked some poor man who stole. He's from inside the walls.
Same story as your grandfather.

Young man with a child and a wife.

JACOB: I'll pray for them.

HILDE: Save your prayers.

JACOB: The child is innocent.

HILDE: If you'd stayed he'd have no need for your piss-poor prayers.

JACOB: Why him?

HILDE: He's a family man. Need a man who's just. They proclaimed it to the town. Who you were, what you did. Town criers went out.

She gets close to him.

Walked the streets saying you were the man who had no justice in him. Said you'd abandoned your home. Said you went about with murderers and thieves.

Your name's shit in the gutter.

JACOB: My name matter's for nothing. You are healer. It is good.

A while.

Could you untie me.

She goes behind him.

She unties him.

He hugs her.

She doesn't hug back.

Eventually she steps back from him.

HILDE: Take your shirt off.

Jacob I need to wash you.

He takes his shirt off.

He is covered in blood.

She looks at it.

They do to you?

JACOB: Nothing I haven't done.

She dips the cloth in the bucket.

She washes him.

A long silence as she washes him.

Will there be a crowd tomorrow?

HILDE: Yes.

JACOB: Will you watch?

HILDE: D'you want me to?

JACOB: D'you want to?

HILDE: I think I must.

A while.

JACOB: When I came through the gate, into the square, did they do to me?

A man struck me down. Then it's dark.

HILDE: You were on a cart. They carried you through the gates.

Crowds beat their fists on you.

JACOB: You see?

HILDE: Yes.

JACOB: You strike?

HILDE: Never.

Turn round.

He turns round.

She washes his back.

He turns.

I've a baby in me.

He turns.

He looks at her.

JACOB: A child?

HILDE: Your child.

JACOB: Our child.

HILDE: Yes.

JACOB: Do they know?

Do town know?

HILDE: Not showing yet.

JACOB: They'll know soon.

And when they know, when they see that child, they'll know it's mine.

HILDE: Mine as well.

The healer.

JACOB: A child.

HILDE: I'd've put a crib near the fire. Built it myself.

JACOB: You'd've shown me the tree.

HILDE: You'd've cut it down, I'd cure the wood.

JACOB: Hung flowers over the door.

HILDE: Took down that wall. Build out.

JACOB: We'd've made a castle in the air.

HILDE: Many things we'd've done.

JACOB: But you heal now.

She washes him.

You should leave.

HILDE: Run?

JACOB: No. Leave.

I ran.

You leave.

HILDE: Go where?

JACOB: Follow the road through the forest.

Say your husband died and you left.

The baby is of that wedding.

Forget all this.

HILDE: Half a truth in that.

JACOB: Don't tell the child about me.

Don't want them to know me.

I'll know them, 's enough.

Say a prayer for them now and wherever I go.

HILDE: Close your eyes.

He closes his eyes.

She washes his face.

She finishes washing his face.

JACOB: Do I look?

HILDE: Clean enough.

JACOB: You won't watch?

HILDE: I won't.

JACOB: And our child?

HILDE: I will tell them their father is Jacob the healer.

JACOB: Will you leave?

HILDE: They'll grow here. In the shadow of those walls. In a house I have built with the men and women outside on land they own.

Going nowhere without a fight.

She picks up the bucket.

JACOB: Hilde.

She stops.

Need to tie me up.

She puts the bucket down, goes to him, ties him up.

HILDE: Tight?

JACOB: Fine.

She faces him.

She kisses him.

She spits on her hand, rubs her thumb in it, puts her thumb on his forehead.

HILDE: Now you're properly clean.

She picks up the bucket.

JACOB: Go well.

HILDE: I will.

Lights.